Restoring Hope and Trust

This book has been made possible, in part, by the generosity of the Kate Sidran Family Foundation.

Restoring Hope and Trust

AN ILLUSTRATED GUIDE TO MASTERING TRAUMA

Lisa Lewis, Ph.D.

Kay Kelly, M.S.W., LSCSW

Jon G. Allen, Ph.D.

Sidran Institute Press
BALTIMORE, MARYLAND

This book is designed to provide information in regard to the subject matter covered. It is sold with the understanding that the publisher and the authors are not engaged in providing psychological or professional services through this medium. If such professional advice or service is required, the services of a competent professional should be sought. The purpose of this workbook is to educate, inform, and enlighten persons who wish to use psychoeducation tools for self-understanding, or those who may be working with such individuals professionally. The authors and Sidran Institute Press will have neither liability nor responsibility to any person or entity with respect to any loss or damage caused, or alleged to be caused, directly or indirectly, by the information in this book.

Printed in the United States of America

9 8 7 6 5 4 3 2 1

LIBRARY OF CONGRESS CATALOGING-IN-PUBLICATION DATA

Lewis, Lisa, 1952–
    Restoring hope and trust : an illustrated guide to mastering trauma / Lisa Lewis, Kay Kelly, Jon G. Allen.
        p.   cm.
    Includes bibliographical references.
    ISBN 1-886968-15-2 (pbk. : alk. paper)
    1. Psychic trauma—Patients—Rehabilitation. 2. Traumatic neuroses—Patients—Rehabilitation. 3. Psychic trauma—Treatment. I. Kelly, Kay, 1954– II. Allen, Jon G. III. Title.
RC552.T7L485 2004
616.85'2103—dc22

                                                                    2004008007

Contents

Restoring Hope and Trust

CHAPTER 1

Introduction

Why Another Book on Trauma?

For many years, we have been conducting psychoeducational groups on trauma with a wide range of clients in treatment at the Menninger Clinic and with their loved ones. When we began this trauma education program, our course spanned many months. We captured the material from this earlier course in the book *Coping with Trauma: A Guide to Self-Understanding*. In recent years, we have sensed the need for a briefer educational curriculum and have developed a ten-session course that captures what we have found to be most important in understanding and learning to master the impact of trauma. Although we continue to conduct the more extended trauma education group, we have found this shorter course to be helpful to people struggling with trauma.

Very often, clients ask us whether we have the material we discuss in our group available in written form. The handouts, outlines, and bibliographies we provide have not fully addressed their interest or responded adequately to their requests. They have been hoping for an actual transcript of the psychoeducational presentations, including the illustrations we drew on the board to depict what we were talking about. This book, then, is the companion text to this short course. It conveys what we have learned directly from and with our clients over years of dialogue in the trauma education groups.

We have found in our groups that the participants relate powerfully to the graphic illustrations. With the assistance of a graphic illustrator, Ms. Susan Corbett, BFA, we have reproduced, in more sophisticated form, the hand-drawn illustrations our clients have found most helpful in our groups. (Therapists wishing to conduct psychoeducational groups have our permission to photocopy the illustrations for personal use. Please give appropriate credit.)

Our initial idea was to direct the book primarily to survivors of trauma, but in the end we targeted three audiences: people struggling to contain and master the spillover of past trauma into their current lives; those who love them and want to have a better idea of how to be helpful; and professionals who would like to conduct psychoeducational trauma groups in their home communities.

Our Theme

Our theme is simple: past trauma often does not remain in the past, but too often spills over into the present. The spillover takes the form of intrusive re-experiencing of the trauma, associated neurophysiological changes, adverse effects on current identity and world view, and depressive mood changes. This spillover can lead individuals to develop and rely on a range of stopgap coping mechanisms, such as alcohol, illegal drugs, or cutting, that are effective in the short run, because they provide relief from tension and distress, but yield diminishing benefits in the long run. Such stopgap coping measures often cause unintended negative effects, such as long-term substance abuse or ongoing deliberate self-injury. The spillover into current relationships can include reenactments of the past trauma in current interpersonal interactions and the potential development of compassion fatigue in loved ones. For the person whose trauma history is continuing to cause problems in current life, this book is to be used as a guide to attaining greater mastery and a sense of well being. Depending upon the degree and range of spillover into your current life, your use of this book can stand alone or can be integrated into a formal treatment process. If you sense that you need more help than this book is providing, do not hesitate to get involved in a treatment process.

Readers should be forewarned that reminders of trauma are the key trigger for symptoms of posttraumatic stress disorder. This book, like other books on trauma, is bound to evoke memories of trauma. We say that with confidence because clients in our educational groups have let us know that the material in our course reminds them of traumatic experience as they listen and participate. Thus, like any form of trauma treatment, reading about trauma can be stressful even though it is intended to be helpful. We make the point in this book that any processing of traumatic memories—thinking, feeling, and talking about trauma—requires some way of containing the emotional distress it evokes. Thus you may find it best to have professional help as you tackle this material. We understand that entering therapy can be a scary step to take, and yet it is at times a necessary and indispensable part of your recovery process.

How to Use This Book

Ideally, you will read this book no more than one chapter at a time. The chapters are intended to be read in the order they are presented, although you may want to read Chapter 11, on treatment, first. The chapters are concise and we hope they will prompt a process of reflection. We suggest you pace yourself in going through this book, just as you would in your life or in your therapy. Digesting the material slowly will make a big difference in what benefits you derive from it. Trying to rush through it, though an understandable desire, will not be helpful. We endorse psychiatrist and trauma therapist Richard Kluft's maxim, "The slower you go, the faster you get there." If you stop your reading in the middle of a chapter, we would encourage you to repeat the mindfulness exercise when you resume.

MINDFULNESS EXERCISES

We have found in our educational groups that reading and discussing a daily meditation or starting with a mindfulness exercise (Linehan, 1993) helps the participants to engage more fully and productively for the remainder of the session. Daily meditation readings, or mindfulness practice, help to get us calm, grounded, and more fully present in the moment. This preparation is important because the more grounded you are in the present moment and the calmer you are, the more likely you will be able to reflect in a productive way on any triggered memories rather than feel overwhelmed by them. If you would prefer to read a daily meditation rather than do the mindfulness practice at the beginning of each chapter, we are entirely in support of that. One daily mediation book we have found quite helpful is *The Language of Letting Go,* by Melody Beattie. It is part of the Hazeldon Meditation Series and is readily available. Or you might have a favorite book of your own.

SELF-STUDY QUESTIONS

Consistent with research findings, we have observed that homework, done in small installments, increases learning and retention over time. Consequently, we have included questions for thought at the end of each chapter. The questions are a form of focused journaling, which studies have also shown can be beneficial. Responding to the Self-Study Questions also helps you to make what you learn in each chapter more personally relevant.

With these preliminary introductions completed, let's begin the process of learning about mastering the impact of trauma.

CHAPTER 2

What Is Trauma?

MINDFULNESS EXERCISE *Sit in a relaxed position with your feet on the floor. If you are comfortable doing so, close your eyes, but otherwise let them rest on a neutral spot. Notice your breathing, allow your mind to become your breath. Follow your breath deeply into your lungs and follow it back out, leaving your body. As you breathe in, count slowly. As you breathe out, think "peace." Do this three or four times. When your mind wanders, simply bring it back gently to your breath.*

Defining Trauma

In everyday life, we use the word "trauma" to describe the negative emotional impact a life event has had on us. For example, if a boyfriend or girlfriend we love dearly breaks off a relationship, causing us pain, we say, "This is traumatic!" In this book, more specifically, we think of trauma as the lasting negative effects of going through tremendously stressful experiences. Often at the heart of such experience is feeling extremely frightened or overwhelmed and utterly alone. When the effects are lasting, we say the person has been "traumatized." Developing posttraumatic stress disorder is the clearest example of being traumatized.

For formal psychiatric diagnosis, we follow the diagnostic criteria set out by the American Psychiatric Association in the *Diagnostic and*

Statistical Manual, fourth edition (DSM-IV). This manual contains the criteria for all psychiatric diagnoses, including posttraumatic stress disorder, or PTSD. PTSD is not the only psychiatric condition to result from exposure to trauma, but it is in many ways the proto-typic trauma-related condition. PTSD first appeared in DSM-III in 1980, following the end of the Vietnam War, when mental health professionals saw large numbers of traumatized military personnel. Prior to 1980, the condition was referred to as shell shock, combat fatigue, or combat neurosis. But in 1980, the condition of PTSD was formally coined and recognized and, since then, the definition of trauma by the American Psychiatric Association has been more clearly spelled out.

As is true with the majority of diagnoses in the DSM, the definition of trauma includes both objective and subjective aspects. The objective aspect of trauma is observable or measurable by others—how an event looks from the outside. The subjective aspect involves the individual's inner experience—how it feels on the inside. Also as is true for most DSM diagnoses, each condition is defined by several categories of objective and subjective events or symptoms. To meet the criteria for the condition the individual must have a specified number of those symptoms from each category. For PTSD, category A covers exposure to potentially traumatic events and includes both objective and subjective features. A traumatic event is defined as one in which the person experienced or witnessed an event that "involved actual or threatened death or serious injury, or a threat to the physical integrity of self or others" (objective) and which involved "intense fear, helplessness, or horror" (subjective).

As you can see, this objective aspect of traumatic events is defined somewhat narrowly. There are many adverse life events, such as verbal abuse, cruelty, or emotional neglect, that do not threaten physical integrity, yet these experiences also may result in posttraumatic symptoms.

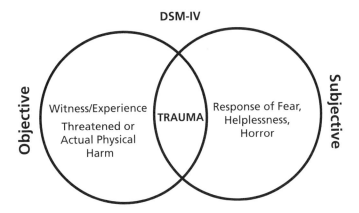

There are, unfortunately, all too many life events that meet even this narrow definition of potentially traumatic events. The following is a partial list:

- experiencing or witnessing physical abuse or violence
- experiencing or witnessing sexual abuse
- rape
- assault
- kidnapping
- automobile, airplane, or train accidents
- natural disasters
- fires
- terrorist attacks
- war
- severe neglect

All of the above meet the objective criteria for potentially traumatic events: they involve actual or threatened damage to one's physical integrity or life or the witnessing of such damage being done to another. If the individual's response involves one of helplessness, fear, and horror, then the subjective criterion is also present and the event is one that may be defined as potentially traumatic.

Not everyone who is exposed to potentially traumatic events develops a psychiatric disorder. You might feel horrified at the sight of a violent crime but not be traumatized in the sense of having nightmares about it and being afraid to leave home months later. At the other extreme, you might experience an empty threat (say, a robber claims to have a gun and wants your money but turns out be unarmed and says later that he would never have hurt you), but if you believed in the moment that your life and physical integrity were threatened and in the balance, then this too would be a potential trauma.

For the people who do experience lasting adverse effects to exposure to trauma one result may be PTSD, which boils down to re-experiencing the trauma in your mind long after the events are past.

DSM specifies three types of symptoms of PTSD that may result from experiencing traumatic events.

- First, you may reexperience the events in the form of flashbacks and nightmares (see Chapter 3).
- Second, you may avoid situations that remind you of the trauma or you may just feel numb.
- Third, you may struggle with a high level of physiological arousal and feel anxious and hypervigilant much of the time.

If this pattern of symptoms is severe enough to cause significant distress or to impair your daily functioning, and the symptoms last more than one month, a diagnosis of PTSD may be justified.

Responses to Trauma

As we said, not everyone who is exposed to a potentially traumatic event goes on to develop symptoms. Think for a moment. What percentage of the adult population has been exposed to one or more potentially traumatic events as defined by DSM? Probably around 80 percent! Of those who have been exposed, depending on which study you look at, about 6–12 percent go on to develop PTSD. Others may not develop PTSD but may show signs of depression instead. Others may cope by engaging in substance abuse. Still others may develop no psychiatric symptoms. Why? Why is the response to trauma so varied?

Below are a few of the factors that contribute to the development of a psychiatric disorder in the wake of extreme stress. Let's take each of these contributing factors in turn and talk more about them.

THE DOSE-RESPONSE EFFECT

The "dose" of trauma can be looked at in two ways:

- The severity of the trauma in a given event
- The quantity of traumatic events experienced.

The more severe the traumatic events you are exposed to, the more likely you are to develop symptoms of a psychiatric disorder. The greater number of traumatic events you are exposed to—the more doses of trauma you receive—the more likely you are to develop a psychiatric disorder. Think of alcohol: the more you drink, the more intoxicated you become. An example will illustrate.

"Jenny," a woman in her 50s, was sitting in her car on a country road, stopped at a railroad crossing while a train was passing.

The crossing gate was lowered and the lights were flashing. She looked into her rearview mirror and watched a truck advancing down the road. The truck did not seem to be slowing, and Jenny began feeling quite anxious. The truck driver suddenly did apply the brakes but was not able to stop before bumping into the back of Jenny's car. She was seat-belted and was jostled forward, but did not get pushed into the gate. After exchanging insurance information with the driver of the truck, Jenny went on about her business. Over the next few days, she began to experience a number of bothersome symptoms—headaches, irritability, difficulty sleeping, poor concentration, and forgetfulness. Jenny went to her family doctor who said, "Even though your head did not strike anything and there was no loss of consciousness, it is possible you had a concussion. I'll send you for a brain scan and to a specialist for neuropsychological testing."

After interviewing Jenny and doing the neuropsychological testing with her, the specialist let her know he was not finding evidence of brain injury but rather PTSD. Jenny said, "You've got to be kidding me. I grew up in a home with a father who was alcoholic and would fly into unpredictable rages and beat on me and my mother and sisters. By the time I was 16, I was big enough to fight back. My mother was afraid we were going to do each other serious damage, so she signed the papers for me to join the Army early. The Army gave me nursing training, and I pulled two tours of duty in Vietnam. Seven years ago my 14-year-old son committed suicide. And you want to tell me that a minor fender bender gave me PTSD?!" The doctor responded that it was precisely because of all the prior traumas that the stress of what turned out to be a minor car accident (although it had had the potential to be quite serious) could cause her to develop symptoms of PTSD.

This is what we mean by the dose-response relationship. The more traumas you are exposed to or the more severe the trauma is, the more likely you are to develop symptoms of a psychiatric disorder. Life holds enough that we have no control over, so we encourage you to avoid exposing yourselves to highly distressing events you do have control over. If watching violent movies upsets you, it is best not to watch them. If watching the news on TV significantly distresses you, do not watch it.

AGE AT EXPOSURE TO TRAUMA

Age also can influence the impact of trauma in two ways. Trauma experienced at a young age has strong effects on

- early brain development and
- later identity.

The first has to do with normal brain development. The brain doubles in volume by the end of the first six months, and it doubles again by the end of the fourth year. Brain development continues well into early adulthood. This is a big part of why we humans have such a long period of dependency on our parents and other caregivers. One implication of this extended period of brain development is that children naturally think very differently than adults. Young children are egocentric; they think the world revolves around them. For example, "If Mommy hurts Daddy it's my fault." Young children also think concretely. They have difficulty understanding complicated reasons for others' behavior. They can't think, for example, "Daddy is hitting me, but it's not my fault: he's really mad at his boss at work," or "He's mad because he has depression or the disease of alcoholism." Children who are exposed to trauma are likely to draw conclusions that attribute the cause to themselves and are more global: "Daddy hits me because I'm bad."

A second way age can play a role in the impact of trauma is that earlier trauma can affect later development. As we will discuss further in Chapter 6, trauma can influence your identity development, the level of trust you have in others, the way you relate to others, and your view of the world. Trauma is horribly painful no matter when it happens in the life span but, all other things being equal, trauma in childhood has a potentially heavier impact owing to its influence on development.

LEVEL OF SOCIAL SUPPORT

Another factor that can have a big impact on how severely and how enduringly trauma will affect a person is the amount of social support the traumatized individual receives in the immediate hours and days after the traumatic event. The presence of other people we trust and who are kind can help replace the experience of terrible vulnerability with a sense of restored safety. That is why we think of traumatic events as those in which the person feels frightened and alone. The presence of people who listen with kindness can help us make sense of what happened, preventing us from arriving at conclusions that shake our sense of self and the world to its core. The presence of people who soothe us can help calm our nervous system that was sent into overdrive by the trauma. Any way you look at it, having people who are kind and compassionate can make a huge difference—at any point after trauma.

INTERPERSONAL VS. IMPERSONAL TRAUMA

To some extent, trauma that was interpersonal and intentional (for example, being beaten by a spouse) can have a greater impact than trauma that was impersonal and accidental (for example, surviving a hurricane). The closer your relationship with the perpetrator of the abuse, and the more the relationship should be a caring and loving one, the more potentially corrosive the impact. Being abused by a parent, sibling, spouse, or friend can warp your sense of what loving relationships are. Being traumatized by someone who should love you can make you feel unlovable and can erode your capacity to trust (see Chapter 9).

TEMPERAMENT

Our temperament also influences how we respond to stressful events. Temperament refers to our inborn personality characteristics, our nature. Some kids are naturally more active, others more quiet. Some kids are naturally more sociable, others more introverted. Psychologist Jerome Kagan has written extensively on one particular temperament dimension, anxiety-proneness, that reflects how we respond to novel or unfamiliar situations.

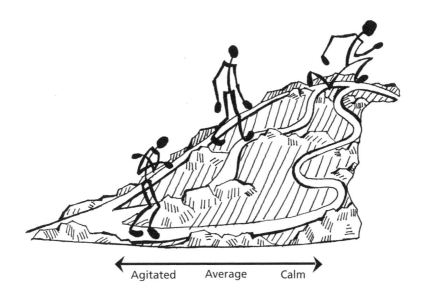

Agitated   Average   Calm

At one extreme are children who become highly agitated when exposed to something or someone new. These are the children who cry and physically cling when left at day care the first few days. They may spend those first days standing against the wall, fearfully watching the children playing around them and perhaps crying occasionally. Once such children have grown familiar with the new environment, they begin to interact normally. At the other end of the continuum are children who respond no differently to a new situation than a familiar one; the world is their oyster. When dropped off at day care the first day, they jump right in and interact freely from the start.

Kagan has found that the children who become agitated when exposed to novelty have a lower threshold for central nervous system arousal (see Chapter 5). These anxiety-prone children are especially fearful and therefore more vulnerable to being traumatized by frightening events. They react more frequently and intensely to stress.

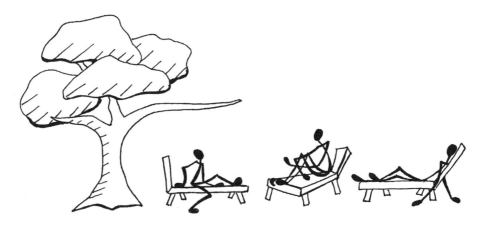

The above illustration shows different degrees of anxiety-proneness. This trait is linked to an individual's customary level of emotional arousal. Depending on where you are on the continuum, your resting level of arousal—how alert, tense, and activated you are—varies. The "world is my oyster" person (shown at the right) has a low resting level of arousal. The person in the middle of the continuum is a little more activated. The person at the easily agitated end of the continuum is fairly tense and activated in routine, everyday life situations.

Because our resting level of activation varies depending on where we are on this temperament spectrum, we do not all react the same to stressful or potentially traumatic life events. It takes less to get the temperamentally anxious person to a state of terror than it does to get people in the middle or the other end of the continuum into that state. Because a response of terror is the subjective aspect of the DSM definition of trauma, individuals with an anxious temperament are more prone to being traumatized.

The match or mismatch of the temperaments of the child and parental figure can also make a difference. If the child's temperament is at the far left of the continuum above, and the parent's is at the far right, attunement and empathy can be more difficult. For example, the child becomes jittery and tearful and pleads not to have to give a piano recital at school. The parent cannot relate to this level of fear in response to a simple, elementary school piano recital and says, "Why are you making such a big deal of this?" Not only does the child feel ashamed of his or her emotions and angry at the parent, but also the child does not learn from the parent valuable coping and self-soothing skills.

So there are a variety of factors that make it more or less likely that someone will develop a psychiatric disorder following exposure to trauma: trauma dose (high to low), age (younger or older), the amount of soothing social support present (none to quite a lot), whether the trauma is interpersonal or impersonal, whether the trauma is intentional or accidental, and temperament (anxious to calm).

Learning to Mentalize

We have looked at factors that influence your vulnerability to developing a psychiatric disorder following exposure to traumatic events. In addition to the factors that we have already discussed that can *reduce* vulnerability, we want to mention another: resilience—that is, the capacity to cope effectively with stress and hardship. Here we wish to introduce a new concept that relates to resilience: the capacity to mentalize.

Our colleague British psychologist Peter Fonagy has shown how mentalizing helps children and adults cope with trauma. Mentalizing involves being aware of mental states in oneself and others—feelings, needs, desires, beliefs, attitudes, and so forth. When we mentalize, we make sense of our own actions and the actions of others. We are able to have distance from our emotional mind and bring more rational, clearer ideas about our earlier experiences to the fore. When children simply blame themselves for being mistreated, they are not mentalizing. When adults turn to alcohol instead of understanding and coping with distressing feelings, they are not mentalizing. We hope that reading this book will help you mentalize—make sense of your emotional experience. If you strengthen your mentalizing ability, you will be less prone to self-blaming about trauma and you will develop an increased resilience. We will be using the concept of mentalizing throughout.

The Chinese symbol for crisis is made up of two symbols, one meaning "danger" and one meaning "opportunity." As horrible as trauma is, it is common, and it does hold potential opportunities for growth when the ingredients necessary for mentalizing are present. Consider the following example:

Viktor Frankl was a psychiatrist who was imprisoned in a Nazi death camp. He tried to hide the manuscript for his book in the lining of his coat but it was found and destroyed. Dr. Frankl survived the concentration camp, though many of his friends and relatives did not, and he emigrated to the United States. He re-wrote his book, entitled *Man's Search for Meaning.* He is the father of existential psychiatry. He said that one of the conditions under which one is more likely to earnestly search for meaning is times of great suffering.

Self-Study Questions

1. What traumatic events have influenced your life? Write only as much as you can without feeling too emotionally upset.

2. What factors increased your risk of developing a psychiatric disorder as a result of your trauma?

3. What factors decreased your risk of developing a psychiatric disorder?

CHAPTER 3

Intrusive Symptoms

MINDFULNESS EXERCISE *Sit comfortably with both feet on the floor. As with all mindfulness exercises, whenever you notice your mind wandering, just gently bring it back. Take a slow, deep belly breath and let it out even more slowly. As you breathe out, imagine the word "compassion" written in your mind. See it written in a color you associate with compassion. Now, as you breathe out again, imagine that your breath carries compassion with it and that compassion is gently permeating all the things, animate and inanimate, around you in the room. And with each breath, the wave of compassion spreads further to envelop all things and creatures in the building where you are, then all things in the neighborhood, and then all things in your community. By the time you have taken ten breaths, you and all in your community will be wrapped in this soft veil of compassion.*

Traumatic and Nontraumatic Memories

To lead into the topic of intrusive re-experiencing of trauma, we would like you to try a little (nontraumatic) experiment. Close your eyes for a moment and try to remember what you ate last night for dinner. Once you have that memory, open your eyes and continue reading this.

When you remembered what you ate for dinner, did it suddenly feel like you were back eating dinner all over again? Before we asked you to remember what you ate for dinner, were memories of dinner last night entering your mind unbidden and unwanted? Probably your answer to these questions is "No." Nontraumatic memories sit in our memory banks and are pulled up when we want them and put back when we are done thinking of them. But traumatic memories are very different. They intrude into our mind and our current experience even when we don't want them to, and often they won't go back on the memory shelf when we want them to.

How Traumatic Memories Intrude

What are some of the ways memories intrude? During sleep, you might have nightmares in which you re-live the trauma, sometimes vividly enough that you are startled awake, in a panic and disoriented. During waking life you may have a full-blown flashback where the current reality becomes completely replaced by the reality of the past trauma. An example will help to illustrate:

"Louis" was undergoing psychotherapy at a VA hospital in the mid-70s, soon after the end of the Vietnam War in which he had been involved in combat. He was talking with his therapist about how he had been struggling even before the war to have his loving feelings temper his hateful feelings, wishing to channel his angry and hateful feelings in constructive directions. It was an important topic and he was quite absorbed in it. As he spoke, he made drawings to illustrate how his combat experiences had even further widened the gulf between his love and his hate. After combat, he had greater difficulty not letting his hateful feelings and impulses spill over into destructive actions. At that point, a door closed in the hallway and made a fairly loud, sharp sound, echoing in the linoleum-floored hall. Louis seemingly levitated into the air and over the back of his chair, rolling onto his belly and crawling on his elbows as though holding a gun and strafing the room with bullets. He crawled, "shot," and rolled in evasive maneuvers. It took several minutes of the therapist repeating his name, the date, and their location before he was able to return to the present. For those minutes, he was back in the jungle of Vietnam. It was all that he was seeing, hearing, smelling, and feeling.

Sometimes the memory intrusions are less complete than a full-blown flashback. Perhaps just a small facet of the trauma intrudes — a sight, a sound, a physical sensation, the feeling of terror, a smell, or the sudden impulse to flee, fight, or freeze. But all intrusive phenomena have this in common: no matter how complete or partial, they evoke significant emotional distress with feelings of terror, vulnerability, and helplessness. Some people have described it as feeling like you are losing your mind and "going crazy."

Avoiding Intrusive Memories

It is no wonder, then, that you do whatever you can to get the intrusive experiences to stop. It only makes sense to want to avoid them. Some ways of avoiding the intrusive memories are quite straightforward.

- You learn to avoid situations that trigger them.
- You stop talking about anything even remotely close to the trauma.
- You avoid doing things that trigger the intrusions.
- You may even repress the memories and be unable to recall them even when you try to.
- You may try to turn off your feelings in an effort to avoid the panicky feelings evoked by the intrusive re-experiencing.

Intrusive

Traumatized

Avoidance

Unfortunately, all these avoidance maneuvers carry a price. The avoidance may make your life get smaller and smaller. Numbing your feelings may involve a decrease in desirable feelings too; you may feel less pleasure and feel more detached or estranged from others. You may feel less love for others even when you know intellectually that you love them. And there is often a paradoxical effect: the more you try to avoid the intrusive experiences, the more they come to mind, and the more you try to avoid. For example, what happens when you are told: "Do not think of a pink elephant. No matter what else you think of do not think of a pink elephant"? For nearly all of us, the harder we try not to think of a pink elephant, the more the image of a pink elephant pops up in our mind. This is the intrusive-avoidance cycle pictured above.

Lifestyle of Avoidance

When these straightforward ways of avoiding don't work well enough, or at all, you might develop a lifestyle based on avoidance. Specifically, traumatized persons often get on a fast-paced, run-run-run, go-go-go lifestyle.

In essence, they max out on whatever talent or talents they have. If they are good students, they study, study, study, get a scholarship to a university, and do their absolute best scholastically. If they are good athletes, they work out for long hours, try out for the team, and strive to make themselves indispensable team members. If they are talented black sheep, they find increasingly spectacular ways of messing up and creating chaos. But here is the rub: this frenetic, driven pace is motivated primarily by avoidance. It is as if they are saying, "Get me as far away from the misery and shame and terror of my traumatic past as you can." And, maybe even less consciously, they are saying "I can't take a moment to stop and sit with myself because I will be flooded with feelings or images or thoughts related to the trauma." And because the main motivation is avoidance, the accomplishments feel like they are slapped on from the outside—hollow and somehow not genuine. The motto is "You are only as good as your last success." And like Satchel Paige's quote, you can't look back because the past might be gaining on you. So you cannot savor your accomplishments, because stopping long enough to savor the pleasure feels dangerous. And, despite your talents and accomplishments, you may feel like a charlatan: somehow the world simply hasn't found you out yet for who you truly are—"whew, tricked them again."

And so you may be locked into a run-run-run lifestyle. The problem is that as long as we are living and breathing, we encounter stress, loss, and perhaps further trauma. So when that inevitable stress comes, you cope the only way you have ever known: you pick yourself up, dust yourself off, and keep moving. There is no time for reflection, for working through, for taking a hiatus to heal and grow. Meanwhile, you are running closer and closer to empty.

The Last Straw

Then there is another stressor or loss followed by a crash. You and the people close to you are often baffled. After all you have accom-

plished, and all of the trauma you have endured, how could something as relatively small as a car accident, or a job loss, or a household move bring you to your knees? You were the one who was so strong, who had it all together, who had weathered bigger losses and traumas and emerged seemingly unscathed. Yet, if you look closely at that last stressor, the last straw, you may find three things:

- It is symbolically linked to the trauma you have been running from (for example, undergoing surgery might be symbolically connected to a previous assault).
- It may be linked to past trauma by common emotions: fear, helplessness, and feeling out of control.
- It may produce a sense of feeling trapped, which may be a sufficient connection to past trauma to evoke a response.

The present may be symbolically connected to the past in other ways as well. One of the women in our psychoeducational trauma group experienced an "aha" moment as she watched us draw and talk about the above figure.

"Amy" had grown up in a home with an alcoholic father who would fly into unpredictable rages and beat her, her siblings, and her mother. Amy was a good book learner. She studied hard, got an academic scholarship to the state university, then worked nights to become a certified public accountant. She often represented clients who were in a contested situation with the Internal Revenue Service. In her most recent case, from her perspective, the IRS had started playing hardball for what she viewed as trumped-up infractions. They audited her office books and her personal tax returns, then confiscated some of her office equipment along with many of her husband's and children's possessions. It was at that point that Amy had a "nervous breakdown" and came to the clinic. As she sat in group with us that day she said, "Now I get it. The IRS was Big Daddy. They were fighting dirty just like my dad did, hurting not just me but my family too." She then understood that this final stress was the last straw, because it was symbolically similar to the initial trauma. It pulled the trauma up out of her past, smack into her present. It wasn't so much the situation with her client's case that brought her down as it was the childhood physical abuse that had been trawling along behind her all these years.

This is the essence of what we call the "90/10 reaction." It is when 10 percent of the current reality bears enough similarity to the past trauma that it pulls the other 90 percent out of the past and right into the present. You go into full fight/flight/freeze mode as though the past trauma was present again. But because the trauma is not really present, the usually innocuous 10 percent in the present moment receives the full force of your stress reaction. We will talk more about the 90/10 reaction in Chapters 4 and 9.

It is best to refrain from using your crash as just a space to catch your breath before you start running again. You'd be better off to use it as a time to take stock, to begin to learn something new—new ways of coping, understanding, and relating. We will talk more about that learning process in Chapter 11.

Private vs. Public Self

The drawing above depicts the big split between the public self and the private self. Despite your accomplishments and how you are viewed in others' eyes, internally you often feel as bad and helpless as you did when the trauma was going on. This split between your private and public self often mirrors the split in the trauma situation. If your trauma involved abuse in childhood, often the community you lived in knew nothing about it. Interpersonal trauma usually is carried out in secret. The family might look just fine, even exceptional, to everyone in the community. But behind closed doors, abusive relationships are being acted out.

The Value of Emotions

This run-run-run, go-go-go diagram puts everything we have been talking about so far in this chapter together in one picture. Months and years of relying on avoidance to calm yourself can cut

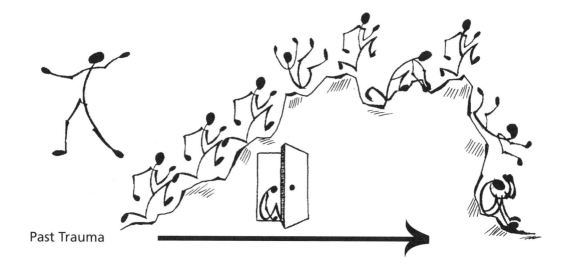

Past Trauma

you off from feelings and emotions. You may have become so afraid of the intensity and disruptive power of your emotions that you have tried, with reasonable success, to kill your emotions off, to live like Mr. Spock on "Star Trek." This is totally understandable. Yet, the best goal is not to rid yourself of emotions (even if that were possible) but rather to increase your ability to tolerate and to regulate your emotions. Our brain is hard wired to produce emotions because emotions are adaptive. Emotions are like e-mail messages to ourselves, and we want to receive them because they carry important information and meanings.

> You may have heard of individuals who have a rare congenital disorder where their skin and other organs contain no pain receptors. They could be leaning against a hot stove and not know it until they look down and see burns on their body. Trying to live without emotions carries the same risk of being oblivious to the impact of life on us.

As we begin to reconnect with our emotions, it is good to keep it simple. J P FLAGS is an acronym that can help:

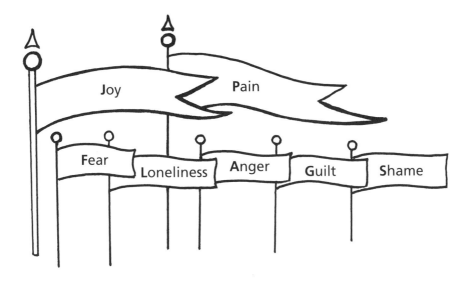

Nearly all types of emotions can be captured by J P FLAGS. If I said I was feeling humiliated, that would fit with shame. If I said I was feeling irritated or frustrated, that would fit with anger. Each of these emotions—if we can let ourselves feel them—carries a potential gift. Let's start with shame.

> An older woman named "Kelly" tells you, "I have never done ANYTHING in my life I am ashamed of." You think she is pretty conceited and arrogant. It is hard to believe anyone could get to the age of five, let alone fifty, without having done many things to be ashamed of.

If we can let ourselves recognize and accept shame, we have the gift of humility. Note that the gift is humility, not humiliation! When we own up to having done something shameful, we know that we are no better than anyone else, we are part of the human race, we are all in this together. We become less judgmental. We have humility.

The gift of guilt is integrity.

I tell you I am going to go with you to the movies tonight. Then someone I've really wanted to make friends with, "Jill," calls and asks me to go out to dinner. I am about to say "Yes," thinking I will call you back and say I am so sorry but I have come down with a really bad cold and must cancel. At that moment, a little voice in my head says, "Hey, wait a minute now, that's not right." I tell Jill I would love to go to dinner with her but can't this evening, because I have already made plans with a friend to go to the movie. I have acted with integrity.

Whenever we feel guilt, we are about to transgress, or already have transgressed, one of our values. We can do two things. We can question the value and see if we want to keep it, if it really fits with our sense of good and bad, right and wrong. If it does not fit, we can modify or replace that value. If we decide to keep it, we can bring our behavior in line with our values and act with integrity. Guilt is like our own internal rudder, helping us to walk our talk.

For those who have interpersonal trauma in their history, anger can be a tough one. Too often, they have seen anger expressed in hurtful, destructive ways.

"Ethan" was afraid to get close to even the faintest forms of anger. His friend "Shellie" had a habit of being late for events he had planned. Rather than tell her that it bothered him, he avoided bringing it up. Shellie kept him waiting an hour once in the cold, but he never said anything.

What is the downside of this avoidance? What gift of anger is lost to those who cannot own it? If we can never let ourselves feel anger, we become doormats. We do not have the gift of assertiveness, the

ability to stand up for ourselves or others in healthy ways. We cannot say, "I would like you to be on time when we have agreed on a time we are going to meet." We cannot say, "I do not want you to talk to me that way." We cannot say, "I'm sorry, but I need to say No to that request at the present moment—I am over-extended as it is."

Have you struggled with a wish to never be alone? Often after trauma, people go to one of two extremes, either always needing to be with someone or never wanting to be with anyone. When we always need to be with someone because we are afraid of bearing the

potential pain of loneliness, we lose a potential gift. The gift of loneliness is solitude. Solitude is the experience of being at peace when alone, having the sense of all being right with us and the world.

Fear is a common experience for people who have been exposed to trauma. Sometimes the fear recurs intensely, even long after the trauma has happened, triggered by seemingly innocuous current events. We come to hate fear. We try to pretend we don't ever feel fear. But that only works for brief periods. We need to learn to distinguish fear that corresponds well with what is happening in the present moment from fear that is more irrational, coming from past and internal sources.

> If lightening strikes the building you are in you feel fear, which is completely normal. Fear creates a natural action tendency: RUN AWAY! So running as fast as you can out of a burning building is a natural and protective response.

But fear of public speaking, driving a car, meeting someone new, telling your therapist something difficult, making a friend, doing a job interview—fear that is intense enough to impair or completely impede doing these parts of everyday life—is a problem. In these instances, if we go ahead and "Just Do It," as the Nike ad says, we reap the gift of courage. Courage is the reward of doing something we

deem the right thing or the necessary thing, despite the fear it causes us.

Sometimes our pain is so intense and feels so unending that we would do anything to rid ourselves of it. Yet, emotional pain is an inevitable part of life. Events happen that cause distress and pain. If we can allow ourselves to feel pain, we reap the gift of sensitivity. We probably have known people who cannot allow themselves to get in touch with their own pain. Our expressions of pain seem to anger

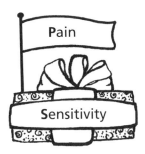

and frustrate them. They exhort us to "Get over it!" and "Put the past behind you!" They may be so afraid of accessing their own emotional pain that they are not able to be sensitive to anyone else's. Sensitivity and empathy are the potential gift of allowing ourselves to acknowledge pain.

And joy is its own gift. Part of what you are probably working on is being able to let yourself have joy. So often after trauma, people feel guilty and undeserving of joy. Or people can be so afraid of letting their guard down that there is no space for joy in their heart and mind. We need to take small steps, let ourselves feel small moments

of joy to build confidence that joy does not heighten our risk of something bad happening to us.

One of the participants in our psychoeducational groups told us about J P FLAGS, it is not our invention. She could not remember where she had learned it and we have been unable to identify its author through computer-based searches of the literature. We have found it valuable to include in our psychoeducational trauma groups and our clients let us know they find it quite helpful. (If the creator of J P FLAGS reads this book, please contact us so that we can appropriately credit you!)

Family Meetings

J P FLAGS can be used in weekly family meetings. A word of caution about this though: If your family is struggling with a lot of pain and is dysfunctional in the sense of expressing too much emotion in ways that are overwhelming, it likely would not be wise to have these family meetings. Family therapy would make more sense. However, if your family generally relates respectfully and reasonably kindly, a J P FLAGS family meeting can be a good way of remaining connected at an emotional level.

Any close family member could be included. Set these meetings at a time when everyone can be there, so that nothing short of an emergency will lead to an absence. Have J P FLAGS on the table. Adults rotate chairing the meeting. The chair has three functions. He or she

- invites everyone to speak using the feeling words of J P FLAGS until they have said enough to share the feelings on their mind and in their heart at the moment (this usually takes one or two minutes for each person).
- helps everyone use "I" language ("I feel angry because you won't let me go to the party at Susan's house this weekend" rather than "You make me angry with all your stupid rules").
- steers the discussion away from problem solving (the sole func-

tion of this type of meeting is to help family members stay connected at an emotional level).

A study done several years ago showed that the average married couple spent only three minutes a week talking about something other than daily life topics! Consciously staying focused exclusively on an emotional level can open communication, reinforce familial bonds, and make each of us feel heard. If necessary a different kind of family meeting can serve the function of solving problems together (sometimes expressing feelings can lead to natural problem solving).

Self-Study Questions

1. How has your past trauma intruded into your present?

2. How have you tried to avoid these intrusions and the emotional pain they cause?

3. Have you gotten into an avoidant, run-run-run, go-go-go lifestyle? If so, in what way?

4. What was your "final straw," and how was it symbolically linked to the past trauma you have been running from?

5. What can you do to begin owning and taking pride in the genuine accomplishments you have made in the course of your go-go-go lifestyle?

6. Do you think having J P FLAGS family meetings would be helpful and, if so, how will you arrange to make them happen?

CHAPTER 4

The 90/10 Reaction

MINDFULNESS EXERCISE *Sit comfortably with both feet on the floor. Let your face rest in a half smile. This is not a big grin; it's a small Mona Lisa smile. It's the kind of smile that might come to you if you were sitting on a park bench and noticed children playing in the distance or heard a bird singing in a nearby tree. Just as our mind controls the movements of our body, the movements of our body send messages back to our brain. A half smile can send a calming, happy message back to your brain. Sit quietly with a half smile, just noticing your breathing, for a few minutes. See if it helps you to feel calmer and more centered.*

A Mountain of Past Trauma

Intrusive posttraumatic symptoms are sometimes caused by what we have come to call the 90/10 reaction. It's a concept we use throughout this book. We know that intrusive symptoms typically are triggered by reminders of trauma. The 90/10 reaction captures this idea.

The 90/10 reaction happens when 10 percent of the emotional response comes from the present, and 90 percent comes from the past. When this happens, you might be criticized for "over-reacting" or "making a mountain out of a molehill." The point of the 90/10 is that there is a real mountain of trauma in the past. This mountain still resides in your memory banks and in your sensitized nervous system. Of course, you can also have a 10/90 reaction when you are mainly responding to some extreme provocation in the present, such as someone screaming at you. Then the reverse may happen: 10 percent of the past adds a little bit of additional fuel to 90 percent of the present. When 90 percent of your emotional response comes from the present, no one will be surprised at its intensity. It's the 90/10s that cause concern to you and others. Learning to separate the current 10 percent from the past 90 percent in the emotional response is an important part of coping with trauma.

Triggers

When the 90/10 reaction happens, you feel emotionally as if the trauma is happening all over again.

"Mary's" teenage son and his friends are watching the Super Bowl at her house. She is happy, as she enjoys having these young people in her home. She fixes a big tray of sandwiches and soft drinks for them and is carrying it from the kitchen to the TV room when she hears a loud burst of cheers from the boys. The noise sends her into a frozen state of panic. She stands immobilized and rigid, her heart pounding in her ears, her eyes wide and fixed. She cannot think straight and feels she is in immediate danger. A few minutes pass, although it feels like an eternity. Gradually, her heart slows, and she regains awareness of her current surroundings. She is in her own home and mentally tells herself she is safe. She proceeds into the TV room, doing her best to be calm and friendly. The boys joke around with her and thank her for the snacks. Later, back in the kitchen, she realizes that the sound of their cheering, of male voices raised in volume, had pulled a particularly painful part of her past into her current experience. The 90 percent of her current emotional response came from her memories of her father's rages when she was a young girl, before he stopped drinking and got on the path of recovery with the help of AA.

The 10 percent of the current reality serves as a "trigger" that brings traumatic memories startlingly into the present. This trigger is usually a sensory experience: a sound, smell, touch, sight, or taste.

In a therapy session with "Soon Ei" we tried to figure out together what had caused her to have a particularly bad episode of dissociation the day before. She had sat in a daze for several hours with no later memory of the time. We looked at the events leading up to the blank time in careful detail. She was walking down a residential street in her neighborhood. It was shortly after 1:00 in the afternoon. It had rained earlier that morning but now the sun was out. She was feeling relaxed, taking in the beauty of the day. She reached a part of the sidewalk that was buckled slightly by the roots of a nearby maple tree. She looked down to make sure she would not trip, and that is the last she remembered until "waking up" on the couch in her apartment nearly four hours later.

What was the 10 percent in that moment that pulled the 90 percent of her painful past into the present? Was it something about a slightly buckled sidewalk? Something about tripping? Then it came to Soon Ei: the trigger was the sight of various colored maple leaves on the sidewalk, wet with rain. The memory pulled from her past was of a neighbor boy harming her in the stairwell of the outside basement steps of her childhood home; the stairwell was concrete and fall-colored maple leaves were stuck to the rain-wetted concrete steps.

Sometimes the trigger is not a sensory perception of something in the environment, but rather a feeling. Often the experience of feeling out of control, helpless, trapped, and vulnerable in a present-day experience propels the past experience into our present. If we look closely at our current experience we can find the 10 percent, the grain of truth, the current spark that ignites the emotional fuel from traumatic memories.

Why Does This Happen?

Why do 90/10 reactions happen? There can be several reasons. Stress pileup is one of them. A pile-up of unprocessed stressful life events can leave us jangled and raw, vulnerable to being triggered. Second, the hypervigilance that frequently follows in the wake of trauma can backfire. In hypervigilance, all your senses are put on high alert. You are continually scanning, scanning, scanning in an effort to notice the first hint of danger. If you can catch the first sign of danger then you will be able to head it off.

Unfortunately, the hypervigilance makes you pay attention to things that most people do not even notice. Because you are already in a state of high anxiety, these stimuli then can trigger you into a 90/10. As one of our patients put it, "My radar is so fine tuned it makes a dinghy look like a destroyer. I go into full attack mode when a simple 'No thank you' is what's called for."

She is referring to the emotional KAPOW described earlier. All emotions are on a continuum. But with trauma and the associated sensitization process, mild levels of feeling can build to fever pitch intensity in a nanosecond. In other words, emotions can be triggers for 90/10s. Normal irritability can escalate into rage. Normal anxiety can escalate into panic or terror. And normal sadness can escalate into despair.

We think you get the picture. This is how some normal emotions can quickly get out of control when the history of the emotion streams into the present-day emotion. What began as a trickle of feeling soon feels like a flood. Because trauma is extreme, you may have extreme emotions and be less aware of the milder or moderate levels of each emotion. One of the steps in decreasing vulnerability to 90/10 reactions is to learn to be aware of your emotions when they are at lower levels of intensity. If you have spent years trying to run from and avoid your emotions, as we described in the last chapter, it takes time to re-develop awareness of them. You will gradually be able to sense milder levels of fear, anger, shame, and so on. It is with these milder levels of emotion that the healthy coping strategies we describe in Chapters 8 and 11 are most effective. These healthy self- and other-regulation strategies we describe are most effective before you reach the "point of difficult return" in terms of the build-up of emotional intensity.

Learning to Recognize and Manage a 90/10 Reaction

The intensity of the emotions experienced in a 90/10 can feel very alarming and often embarrassing. When others say you are too sensitive, at some level, you know they are right. By understanding sensitization, it is possible to be less judgmental and self-critical about this sensitivity. The intensity of the emotion experienced in the present is disproportionate to the current reality. This is the essence of the 90/10. And if we find the 10 percent in the present propelling us into 100 percent emotional intensity, we can learn what in our past is contributing the bulk of the feeling.

The idea of controlling intense feelings is easy to say and hard to do. You may find it nearly impossible to stop the initial burst of intense feeling, although the various ways of managing your emotional arousal that we discuss in a later chapter can lower your general level of reactivity. Even if you cannot prevent or stop this initial burst of emotion, you can learn to gain some control over its course. You can learn to mentalize — to identify your response as a 90/10 and to understand where the additional 90 percent is coming from. This will allow you to begin to calm yourself, to come down from the emotional intensity of the 90/10. With the recognition that you are experiencing a 90/10 comes the realization you are not in current danger. As you become calmer, you will be able to reflect on your experience and its basis in past trauma. This requires your reestablishing a sense of being well grounded in a safe and secure current reality along with a certain degree of confidence in your ability to look into the past without the 90/10 being set off again.

When trauma occurs, you are not only dealing with the emotions of trauma but also the subjective thoughts about the trauma. Taking an observing stance in relation to the traumatic event, that is, studying the emotions and subjective thoughts associated with the trauma, is what we call mindfully noticing and describing, or objective thinking.

Sometimes the capacity to observe mindfully is imparted by doing the reflective work with the help of a therapist. Each time you trace the emotion back through your past to its nodal points in your memory network you rob the past of a bit of its power to flood into your present. We will talk more about this learning process in Chapter 11. Often just considering that you might be in a 90/10 can bring more objective thinking into your experience. This reflective space helps you to be a thinking person who has feelings and un-sticks you from the experience of being consumed and completely filled by emotion.

Self-Study Questions

If you have had several 90/10 experiences, think of one that you can remember happening some months or years ago.

1. What was the 10 percent of the then-current situation that pulled up 90 percent of your past?

2. What might you be able to change about your current living or work environment to lessen similarities to traumatic past environments?

3. Do you notice patterns or themes in your 90/10s? What are they?

4. Who can help you with this? Who can you ask to help you with this?

CHAPTER 5

Somatic Impact: Adaptation Gone Awry

MINDFULNESS EXERCISE *Look around the room you're in. Let your eyes travel neutrally, nonjudgmentally, all the way around the room. Let them come to rest on the object that delights you most. Use your eyes to just notice that object. Observe its color, its shape, its texture. Now put words to what you are noticing: name the color, name the shape, name the texture. Breathe slowly and from your belly as you are doing this. If your mind wanders, just be aware that it has wandered and bring it back to the object in the room. Take a few more good breaths and begin to read this chapter when you feel grounded and centered.*

In this chapter we will be explaining the biology of the stress response in detail. We do this because it can help you to more fully appreciate many of the symptoms, experiences, and behaviors that can occur in people who have been traumatized. At the same time, we acknowledge that the concepts we will be presenting are complex, especially if you do not have some prior background in biology. We will begin by summarizing some key concepts and then we will discuss the biological bases of these concepts more fully. We suggest that you make an effort to understand the key concepts and, if the biology is of little interest, that you skim over it or simply skip to the next chapter.

Key Concepts

We cannot fully understand intrusive posttraumatic symptoms, the 90/10 reactions, without taking into account the role of the body. To a greater extent than we appreciate, emotions are bodily reactions. We are aware of these emotional changes in our body when we have strong feelings. Repeated, extreme stress can sensitize the nervous system, resulting in a persistent change in the way the body responds to stress. Sensitized, it is as if your nervous system is on guard: "The world is dangerous, so I'd better be ready to react in an instant." This strong, nearly instantaneous reaction ordinarily takes the form of fight, flight, or freeze. Understanding how the nervous system has been constructed through evolution to respond this way may help you be more compassionate toward yourself when you have the 90/10 reaction.

Further, understanding how the nervous system and the body generally react to repeated, high levels of fear can help you understand some of your other experiences. Specifically, we know that repeated high levels of fear can impair the functioning of the structures in our brain that allow us to lay down new memories. When such impairment occurs, our memories can become spotty and patchy. If your memory of past trauma is spotty, you cannot necessarily assume that the full memory has been stored in your brain. The more or less complete memory may have been stored and is now inaccessible due to the psychological defense mechanism of repression. On the other hand, it is possible that your brain's ability to store new memories was impaired. Rather than trying to force memories to come, we encourage you to simply work with what you do remember.

We also have come to know that repeated very high levels of fear can have potential impact on the body generally. It can contribute to gastrointestinal problems, muscle and joint pains, headaches, appetite changes, and so on.

The discussion of biology in this chapter is intended to help you to better understand the following key concepts:

- sensitization as it relates to the 90/10 reaction
- how the adaptive nature of the fight-flight-freeze and the floppy immobility response can go awry once PTSD develops
- the potential impact of repeated high levels of fear on memory, and
- the potential impact of repeated high levels of fear and chronic anxiety on the body generally.

If you are interested in the biological details, please read on. Otherwise, simply skip to the next chapter.

Biology of Stress

Deep within the brain are phylogenetically old structures we share in common with other animals. Horses, alligators, dogs, cats, and humans have them. They are part of a system Paul MacLean, a prominent neuroscientist, called the limbic system. The limbic system generates emotions and feelings that prompt adaptive action.

On the surface of the brain is the cortex. "Cortex" means bark or covering, and the cortex of the brain was believed by ancient people to be simply a protective layer like the bark of a tree. We now know that the cortex contains billions of cell bodies of neurons. The cortex is the most recent part of the brain to have evolved, and humans have more cortex than any other animal. Logical processing and reasoning depend largely on the brain's cortex.

If you look at the brain of a rat, it's pretty smooth. The brain of a cat has more humps and valleys, and the brain of a chimpanzee even more. But humans have even more of these humps and valleys, known as gyri and sulci. This is nature's way of packing more cortical surface area into the confined space of the bony inner chamber of the skull. If we took a king-size sheet and spread it out flat, it would cover a lot of the area of the floor. But if we crimped and pleated it carefully, we could get the surface area of that large sheet into a much smaller area of the floor. So humans have much more cortex, especially in the frontal lobes, than other animals, without having to have proportionately bigger heads.

To a large extent, the cortex of the left hemisphere reasons with linear, sequential logic. The right hemisphere, on the other hand, reasons more holistically and spatially. The writer depends heavily on the left hemisphere; the carpenter depends heavily on the right hemisphere. We always use both hemispheres together, for example, when we appreciate both the lyrics and melody of a song.

To illustrate the difference between the two hemispheres, we would like you to mentally solve the following problem: A man bought a slightly used table at a garage sale for 2/3 of what it cost new. He paid $50 for it. How much did it cost new? If you inverted the fraction and multiplied (3/2 x 50 = 150/2 = 75), you were using the linear application of a logical principle that is more characteristic of left hemisphere processing. If you mentally pictured the problem as a column labeled 50 next to a column representing 3 thirds and mentally "saw" that 1/3 = 25 so 3/3 = 75, you were using the spatial application of logic more characteristic of the right hemisphere. It's hard to represent this spatial form of reasoning using language, which involves linear, sequential logic, but we hope you caught the gist of it.

In very general terms, we associate reasoning with the cortex and we associate emotions with the limbic system. There are billions of connections between the neurons in the cortex and in the limbic system, traveling in both directions. So neuroanatomically there are abundant pathways for these regions of the brain to communicate with and influence each other. Yet, sometimes those pathways are not as functionally active as would be ideal. This is especially true in the case of people experiencing trauma. Trauma is an emotionally overwhelming event that functionally can disconnect our ability to think and feel at the same time. We can think without feeling, and we can feel without thinking. Trauma can make it especially hard to do both at the same time.

An example of how our limbic system acts is found in a Disney movie that came out some years ago called "Never Cry Wolf." It is based on a book about an academic scientist who is employed by the Canadian government to determine what is depleting the caribou population.

The government suspects it is wolves. After much hardship, the scientist finally sets up his camp across the pond from a family of wolves. The alpha male wolf watches with ears pricked and eyes alert as the scientist brews pot after pot of tea. Over a few hours, the scientist urinates around the perimeter of the camp. When the scientist is done, the alpha male wolf trots over and, in a few minutes, urinates on the outside of that perimeter. These behaviors are communicating messages. The scientist is sending the message to the wolf "Inside this circle is my space" and the wolf is telling the scientist "I accept that. And outside the circle is my space." Why did they do this? Because the proximity of man to wolf caused the limbic system of each to generate a degree of fear that prompted behavior designed to decrease fear and wariness of each other. Securing territory and having that territorial line accepted decreases fear and increases a sense of safety.

Another, strictly human, example may sound familiar to many of us:

For years, "Ellen" and "Suzanne" co-led a psychoeducational trauma group. They had fallen into a pattern, as people tend to do. Ellen always sat in the chair on the right side of the blackboard, and Suzanne always sat on the left. A new co-leader, "Paul," replaced Suzanne, and when Ellen entered the group room, he was sitting in the chair on the right side of the blackboard. She felt a twinge of uneasiness and went and sat in the left side chair. It didn't feel right. She leaned over and said, "Will you please switch chairs?" He looked at her a bit oddly but, of course, complied. As soon as Ellen sat in "her" chair again she felt at ease.

We humans are animals, too. We establish territory and feel varying degrees of unease or alarm when someone violates our territory. Think about it. How would you feel if your partner got into "your" side of the bed, someone stood "too close" while you were talking with them, someone sat in "your" place at the dinner table, and someone parked in "your" spot in the parking lot? Typically, such events cause us to feel some degree of uneasiness or irritation. Luckily because our response stems from our cortex functioning along with our limbic system we don't generally physically attack the other person or bare our teeth and growl like a wolf.

All these brain structures are there to increase the probability of survival of the individual and the species; that's why they have evolved.

In the figure below, some key structures in the limbic system have been drawn in and labeled: the amygdala, the hippocampus, the hypothalamus, and the pituitary gland. The amygdala plays a key role in what is called fear conditioning. The term, conditioning, refers to a particular type of learning: learning from events that threaten our survival and elicit fear. These can be external events, such as someone approaching with a fist upraised. Or they can be internal events, such as a nightmare or a worsening sense of pressure and pain in the chest and radiating into the left arm and jaw. These events turn on the amygdala.

The amygdala sends a message to the hypothalamus. The hypothalamus is the control center of the autonomic nervous system (ANS). The ANS has two branches. The sympathetic branch increases

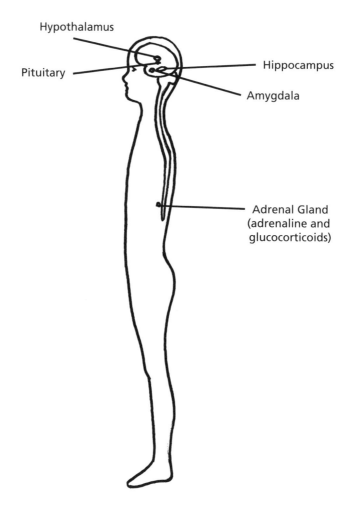

Hypothalamus

Pituitary

Hippocampus

Amygdala

Adrenal Gland
(adrenaline and
glucocorticoids)

arousal and activation. The parasympathetic branch lowers arousal and activation. Like most aspects of our body, these two branches allow for a range of activation. Just like the bicep muscle in our upper arm, when contracted, raises the forearm and the triceps, when contracted, lower the forearm—allowing for a range of physical motion—the two branches of the ANS allow for a range of physiological activation. Ideally, the level of activation suits the environmental demands. We all have listened to someone who is under-activated give a speech while talking in a monotone, putting us to sleep. We all have listened to someone give a talk who is over-activated, with papers shaking in trembling hands, tremulous voice, breaths drawn in shallow gasps, and a tenuous hold on a train of thought. Performance on most tasks is best with the right balance of the two branches of the ANS.

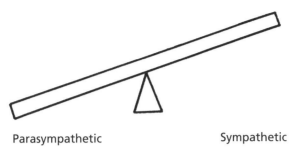

Parasympathetic   Sympathetic

A stalk, called the infundibulum, connects the hypothalamus to the pituitary glad. If we could look up through the roof of our mouth, we would see the pituitary gland dangling at the base of our brain. The pituitary gland has two chambers. One chamber stores hormones that are produced by the hypothalamus and drip down the infundibulum into the chamber of the pituitary. The other chamber contains hormones produced by the pituitary gland. Hormones are chemical substances that, when released, circulate through the bloodstream and exert an effect on a distant organ or organs. The pituitary hormone we will be focusing on is adrenocorticotrophic hormone or ACTH. The adrenocortico part of that word is referring to the cortex of the adrenal gland.

The adrenal glands sit above the kidneys. They produce adrenaline and glucocorticoids that play a key role in the adaptive stress response. The hippocampus has more receptor sites for glucocorticoids than any other part of the brain does. The hippocampus facilitates converting immediate sensory experience into an enduring memory. Memories are not stored in the hippocampus, but without hippocampi, we can lay down no new memories. In the short run, the increase in glucocorticoids allows the hippocampus to create vivid memories.

What do you experience in your body when a big dose of adrenaline is released into your bloodstream? (Remember, adrenaline is a hormone and will affect distant organs. By identifying the changes that occur in your body in response to adrenaline, you can tell what organs are affected by adrenaline.) There are many changes that take place throughout our body in response to adrenaline in our blood stream:

- heart rate and respiration increase
- pupils dilate and sensory acuity generally is increased
- muscle tonus or tension increases
- skin feels cool and often sweaty on the palms and soles
- mental alertness picks up

There is only so much blood in our body, and more of it is being directed to our heart, lungs, skeletal muscles, and brain because each of these organs is working harder.

With only so much blood in our body, less is flowing to our gastrointestinal system from stem to stern, and less is flowing to our skin. These changes are adaptive. With less blood in surface vessels, there will be less bleeding with a superficial injury. You may have heard the term, "scared spitless"—or maybe a related term if you change one letter in the last word. With less blood going to the GI system, the salivary glands are producing less saliva so the mouth feels dry and sticky, and food feels like a lump in the stomach. With enough adrenaline, you might vomit, urinate, and defecate. Because effort needs to go to functions of the body other than digestion, the body empties the GI tract.

What are all these changes in our body gearing us up to do?

In the 1920s and 30s, the physiologist Walter Cannon greatly enriched our understanding of the biological basis of the fight-or-flight response, and he fully appreciated how easily this powerful response could be set off. An example will illustrate.

"Rosita" and I were visiting as our dogs were playing. She had two dogs, a dominant male and a female, both quite large, weighing over 100 pounds each. My dog is about 50 pounds and loves Rosita's female dog. In playing and racing around with her, my dog jumped into Rosita's lap, and her male dog immediately lunged at my dog, baring his teeth and growling deeply. The next thing I knew, I was on the other side of the room with no recollection of intending to get there or of how I got there. The next thing Rosita knew, she was standing over the two dogs, pulling them apart, with no recollection of any intent to do so or how she did so. It was my limbic system, not so much my cortex, that motivated my flight response. Ditto for Rosita's fight response.

We now know that the freeze response is also mediated by this hypothalamic-pituitary-adrenal axis. In the freeze response, muscle tone, heart rate, sensory acuity, and alertness are all high. The response resembles what we did as kids when we played the game of statue: if you were tagged, you froze.

This whole system and the resultant fight-flight-freeze responses have an adaptive potential. By and large, carnivores and omnivores have their eyes on the front of their head. They are highly visual creatures, with their visual systems being especially sensitive to movement. Herbivores, by and large, have their eyes on the sides of their head. This increases their range of peripheral vision. If we went and sat quietly in a field, we would begin to notice the wildlife. We would see rabbits and mice and deer in the field, all with eyes on the sides of their heads, being herbivores. And we would see a hawk or two riding the thermals, making those slow circular passes in the sky. What would the rabbit do if it saw the shadow of the hawk? If you thought, "freeze," you're right. Rabbits that freeze will be more likely to survive, because hawks will be less likely to see them. An example that will be familiar to cat owners may help illustrate:

> I am washing dishes and my cat, Cleo, brings a preying mantis into the kitchen and drops it from her mouth onto the linoleum. Cleo goes into a still crouch. The preying mantis remains motionless. Seconds pass. The preying mantis moves and Cleo pounces, taking the mantis into her mouth. Cleo drops the mantis to the linoleum, then goes back into her still crouch. The cycle repeats. I think to myself, "This cat is a sadist." I scoop up the preying mantis, take it outside, and set it on the branch of a tree where it can be happy. Later in my studies I realize Cleo's behavior had nothing to do with sadism. Like nearly all predators, her visual cortex is highly attuned to detect movement, and movement of a prey animal elicits her predation response.

Scientists recently learned about yet another potentially adaptive response: floppy immobility. In a naturalistic, scientific observation experiment, the scientist observed the behavior of geese and foxes.

Floppy Immobility

If the flock of geese saw the fox approaching at a distance, the flock took flight. If an individual goose noticed the fox when it was somewhat closer, the goose would freeze. If the fox continued to advance, the goose would begin to fight, pecking with its bill and raking with its feet. If the fox took the goose into its mouth, the goose often went into floppy immobility. This is very different from a freeze response. Muscles go limp, eyes look glazed, and heart rate slows—just the opposite of what happens with the adrenaline burst of the freeze response. Geese that went into floppy immobility were three times more likely to survive than geese that continued to freeze or fight. Foxes are predators, not scavengers. The fox had not killed that goose, but it appeared to be dead, so the fox would be likely to drop it and move on. Some minutes later, when the fox had left the scene, the goose would return to normal consciousness and take flight.

The floppy immobility response appears to depend on endogenous opioids, such as endorphins and enkephalins. These are opiates, narcotic-like substances produced by the body. In addition to the effects described above, they have an analgesic (pain-inhibiting) effect, a blessing of nature for beings in a life-threatening situation.

If we are explaining this clearly, you can appreciate the tremendous adaptive value of the fight, flight, freeze, and floppy immobility responses that our neurophysiology makes possible. They are reflexes that evolved to save our skins. We cannot stop our reflexes, but we can learn to take charge of them once they have been triggered. That's why we also have that complicated cortex.

Let's run through it to make sure you understand how this system works and how it is adaptive.

"Ivan" decides he is thirsty and would like to get a latte. He gets into the car, buckles up, and starts driving to the closest coffee shop. On the way, he hears squealing breaks and sees a tractor-trailer traveling in the opposite direction that has blown a rear tire and is weaving erratically back and forth across the lanes. His eyes send this information to the brain. It is an event that threatens his survival, so the amygdala becomes activated and sends a message to the hypothalamus. The hypothalamus sends a message to the pituitary and ACTH is released into the blood stream. The ACTH reaches the adrenal glands, prompting them to release adrenaline and glucocorticoids. He is geared up to fight-flight-freeze and his hippocampus is laying down vivid memories, facilitated by the glucocorticoids.

It is highly unlikely that he would go into *fight* mode, pressing fiercely on the gas and charging toward the truck. He might *flee* by turning the wheel towards the curb. Or he might *freeze,* applying the breaks and stopping the car. Which of these latter responses he would have would not involve a lot of conscious reflection. It would be a reflex. Fleeing or freezing in this situation would be adaptive. Both responses would reduce the odds of a collision, and the freeze would reduce the impact if collision occurred.

But what if the danger is living in a neighborhood with drive-by shootings and robberies and you cannot afford to move to a safer neighborhood? What if the danger is living with a parent who periodically flies into a rage? Will fighting help? Probably fighting will make the situation worse. Will fleeing help? Not if you are a child without the capacity to function on your own. Will freezing help? Maybe sometimes but not always.

What if the danger is in your own mind—recurrent nightmares, flashbacks, and other forms of intrusive symptoms we talked about in Chapter 3? How do you fight, flee, freeze, or get into floppy immobility to cope with any of those?

You can see that there are many modern situations in which this marvelously adaptive system goes awry. We are recurrently jacked up to high levels of sympathetic arousal with no adaptive behavioral outlet. This has an impact on our brain in at least two ways. First, a process of sensitization or kindling can occur in the amygdala. This means that the threshold for firing gets lower and lower. It means that it takes less to get the amygdala to turn on at high intensity and get the whole process started. So, at first it takes 100 percent of the clear and present danger, then only 80 percent, then 40 percent, and so on. This is the neurophysiological basis of the 90/10 phenomenon, where 10 percent of the current reality is similar enough to the past trauma to pull it smack into the present and make us react like it is all happening again, even when it isn't. As we mentioned at the beginning of this chapter, it is as though our amygdala is saying "I'm getting activated a lot. I live in a dangerous world. I'm going to become even more alert and sensitive so I don't miss danger signals and get caught off guard." This process of sensitization also contributes to the hypervigilance and exaggerated startle response that can follow exposure to trauma.

The second process involves changes in the hippocampus that can result from recurrent high levels of activation of the hypothalamic-pituitary-adrenal axis. In the short run, high levels of glucocorticoids facilitate the functioning of the hippocampus in laying down new memories. Over time, however, recurrently high levels of glucocorticoids cause the cells in the hippocampus to shrink. This shrinking process may serve to protect the neurons from further damage. If the level of glucocorticoids remains recurrently high, some neurons in the hippocampus will die. In either case, the ability to lay down new memories is then compromised. This is one of the reasons for caution regarding the accuracy of memory for trauma when the memories are fuzzy, unclear, or very fragmented. Although it is possible that gaps in memory are due to repression (that is, the memory is in there but unconsciously repressed because it is too painful) it is also possible that an elaborate memory was never laid down in the first place. Often, especially when the events happened long ago or early in childhood, all you may have are bits and pieces. Using memory retrieval techniques, such as hypnosis, may enable you to construct more full-fledged memories. But their accuracy will be difficult to determine from the memory itself. You may need to do some detective work if you are so inclined, talking to others in your family, for example, who may know more about the events in question. We, like most therapists, encourage clients simply to work with what they do remember of their trauma and not to try to force the process of remembering.

The possibility of lasting damage to the hippocampus and to memory capacities is certainly reason for concern. Yet, just as we are learning more and more about the possible detrimental effects of stress, we are also learning about the healing power of the brain. The good news is that the process of sensitization in the amygdala and cell damage in the hippocampus is potentially reversible. We used to believe that neurons in the brain had no capacity to replicate DNA and divide: once you lost a brain cell it was a permanent loss. But researchers are finding that cell regeneration does occur in the dentate gyrus of the hippocampus and other places in the brain.

The key to halting the sensitization and neuron damage, and reversing these processes, is in finding ways to stop the recurrent high activation of the hypothalamic-pituitary-adrenal axis. In other words, the goal is to reduce, or ideally eliminate, exposure to ongoing trauma as well as the intrusions of past trauma into the present. This is not easy to do, but it is possible. In addition, we now know that antidepressant medications can stimulate nerve growth factors that help reverse this process and lead to more resilience to stress. We cover these matters in our discussion of treatment in Chapter 11.

Another key to halting sensitization and neuron damage, and reversing these processes, is to abstain from substance abuse. Individuals who have been traumatized may understandably turn to alcohol or drugs in an effort to make the intrusive symptoms stop or quiet down. Unfortunately, over time, many substances of abuse make the sensitization process in the amygdale and the cell death in the hippocampus worse. So, abstaining from substance abuse or misuse is a very important component of recovery.

Another thing to be aware of is the effects of recurrent high levels of sympathetic arousal on the body as a whole. Adrenaline has effects on many organ systems. Thus adrenaline can exacerbate GI conditions such as irritable bowel syndrome or ulcers, contribute to the development of anorexia nervosa, or cause tension headaches or muscle and joint pain. Often these stress-related symptoms do not develop into diagnosable diseases and you may be frustrated if you get the message from your physician that your symptoms are not real. It is dangerous to dismiss your physical symptoms, especially if you do ultimately develop a diagnosable disease that should be treated. If you have the good fortune to work with a primary health care provider you trust, let him or her know of your trauma history and any trauma-related psychiatric diagnoses for which you are in treatment. This will help your health care provider know to consider this in making the proper diagnosis. It will minimize their doing workups

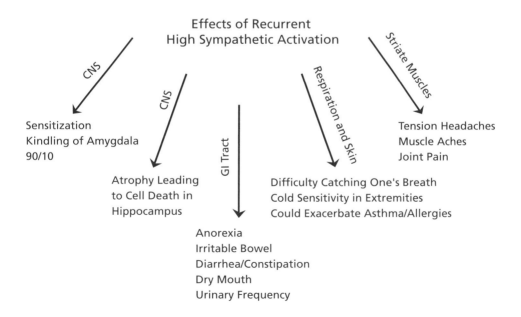

and concluding, "It's all in your head." As we have discussed in this chapter, it is literally all in your head and in your body, which is not the same thing as saying it is imagined.

Self-Study Questions

1. Do intrusive re-experiences of any past trauma cause you to have the kinds of changes in the body associated with the fight-flight-freeze response?

2. If so, what healthy ways have you found of calming and soothing yourself? What other ways might you try?

3. Do you think you have stress-related physical symptoms? If so, what are they?

CHAPTER 6

Identity

MINDFULNESS EXERCISE *Take a moment to become comfortable and settled in your chair, with both your feet on the floor. Take a deep diaphragmatic breath and exhale slowly. As you breathe, notice three things that you can see, such as a wall, picture, window, another person, or a piece of furniture. As you breathe, notice three things you can hear, such as a television or radio, a bird outside, or your breath. As you breathe, notice three things you feel, such as the chair, the floor, your arms on the table, or a sensation of hunger. Take another slow, deep breath and come back to full awareness of what is around you. Note what you experienced with your senses, just recognizing it mentally or writing it down. This mindfulness practice can help when you are dealing with distressing memories from traumatic events in the past or with worries about future events. Mindfulness can help you stay grounded in the present.*

We have been talking about how past trauma can spill over into the present in terms of intrusive memories, the body, and 90/10 reactions. In this chapter we will talk about the spillover of past trauma into our current identity and sense of self. While it is important to recognize the current impact of past trauma on our identity, it is perhaps even more important to recognize that there is more to us than trauma. We will discuss three factors that contribute to our sense of identity:

- biology/genetics,
- social influences, and
- family of origin.

Biological Influences

Let's start with the biological factors. The biological self defines us by the attributes with which we come into the world. What things are we born with that influence our sense of who we are? Take just a minute or two to ponder this question. The following is just a partial list:

- gender,
- race,
- physical attributes (e.g., height, coloring),
- temperament,
- talents and skills,
- vulnerability to illness (e.g., alcoholism, depression), and
- intellect.

We can appreciate how all these factors play a role in our developing sense of self. If I am an African-American female with an IQ of 135 and a height of 5'1", my sense of identity will be very different than if I am a Caucasian male with an IQ of 135, severe dyslexia, and a height of 6'3". Of course, genetic traits interact with our social self by influencing how others respond to us and where we stand in our community. For example: Am I part of a minority group? Do I look very different than most people around me? Is my intelligence significantly different from the people around me? Feeling like the odd one out can lead to anxiety, as the following example illustrates:

> "Demetria" grew up in a northeastern state in a community that was ethnically and racially mixed, but with a large population of persons of Italian, Greek, and Middle Eastern extraction.

Shortly after moving to Kansas, she went with a friend to a Kansas University football game. She found herself feeling anxious and unsettled despite its being a beautiful fall day. Finally, looking around, she realized the source of her anxiety. The most common hair color of the thousands of people in the stadium was blonde. Most people were fair skinned and taller than she was used to. She was now a member of the minority, in terms of her physical appearance.

Social Factors

Next, let's consider the social factors that contribute to our developing sense of who we are. You are shaped and influenced by the people in your social life and your community, especially by the people with whom you identify. Often, with trauma, you are isolated from others outside your family. Still, when you enter school, your skills and talents can lead a teacher or a coach to notice and nourish your special gifts. Take a minute to reflect on your life and the social factors that contributed to your identity. The following is, again, a partial list of contributors to your social self:

- socioeconomic status,
- geographical location (e.g., urban, suburban, rural; region of the country),
- religious affiliation,
- sports team identification,
- club and clique memberships, and
- relationships with teachers.

It's fairly easy to appreciate how growing up on a farm in rural Georgia might lead to the development of a very different sense of self than growing up in New York City. Consider how growing up in one of the poorest versus wealthiest families in the community would make a difference in your sense of self. Think about how having one or two really exceptional teachers who recognize your interests or talents can make all the difference in your sense of who you are.

In the following example, you can see how our frame of reference is strongly influenced by the social factors that contribute to our identity.

> "Linda" grew up in a small town in southwestern Pennsylvania. The community was predominantly lower-middle class. There were people who were poor and rich, but not very many. She moved to the northeast to work on her Masters degree at a small, private, liberal arts college. By being a teaching assistant, she earned a stipend that paid her tuition. The students at the college were allowed to invite a teacher to dinner once a week. One of the students invited her for dinner at the dorm. She was struck that the dining room had round tables with linen tablecloths and napkins, as well as upholstered chairs. The meals were buffet style, not cafeteria style. After dinner the student invited her to see what the dorm rooms were like. Again, she was impressed with the homey and un-dorm-like feel to the rooms. On the student's bureau she noticed a framed photograph of several teenaged girls in pretty, formal dresses. She asked, "Is that your prom picture?" "No that's my coming out ball," the student responded. Thankfully, she did not say it out loud, but Linda's mental reaction was "Wow! These rich people are so liberal! They find out their daughter is a lesbian and they throw her a party!" The social sphere Linda had grown up in did not include the concept of debutante balls, so the term "coming out" had only one meaning to her.

In another example, a student's talent may have been forever undiscovered had it not been for a teacher who nurtured it.

"Shakira" went through K–6th grades unaware of any artistic talent she had. She discovered her gifts when her 7th grade art teacher recognized her skill and talent and began to nurture her in this area. The teacher encouraged her to enter her artwork in shows and contests, many of which she won. She went on to take many more art classes, paint, win awards and scholarships, love art, and grow in a talent that lay dormant until a teacher noticed it in her.

Influence of Family of Origin

Our experiences from early childhood with our family of origin also influence our sense of self—who we are and how we see the world around us. How we were treated in childhood influences how we feel and think along with what we believe about ourselves. We learn and retain these foundations through our lifetime. These ideas are not easy to change, and the process of change will take time. Most of our experiences are a mixture of good and bad, and they affect our sense of goodness and badness.

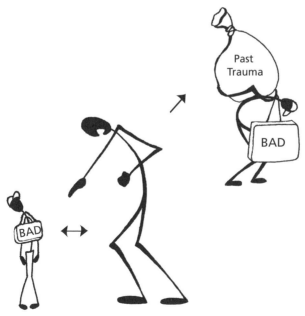

If our parental figures grew up in an environment where bad experiences outweighed the good, they would be likely to pass that on to us. We might get more bad than good messages about ourselves from them. Those bad messages can be given to us in words or in deeds.

As we grow, this experience grows with us unless there are challenges to these beliefs. Our self-experience remains "I'm bad." You may feel that "I'm bad," but you may state your "badness" in other ways:

- "I'm stupid,"
- "I'm to blame,"
- "I'm unlovable,"
- "I'm shameful,"
- "I'm guilty,"
- "I'm undeserving," or
- "I'm never good enough."

These self-experiences can feel like bedrock truths about ourselves. We can feel that our badness is the core of our existence, as unchangeable as our height or our race. Many of our clients have told us that they believe they were born with that sense of "badness." But remember, these feelings, thoughts, and beliefs were learned. They may have been a part of you for quite some time, but badness is not one of the traits we listed under the biological self.

The challenge comes in being open to learning and accepting new experiences. Old beliefs about your inherent badness must be challenged. Responsibility for trauma must be shifted to the appropriate source. Adding new, good experiences and positive beliefs about yourself must be a focus in shrinking the badness.

Others may say they think well of you, and you may dismiss their opinions, thinking they don't know the real you. Often, others can see us more accurately than we see ourselves. Trauma can lead to highly

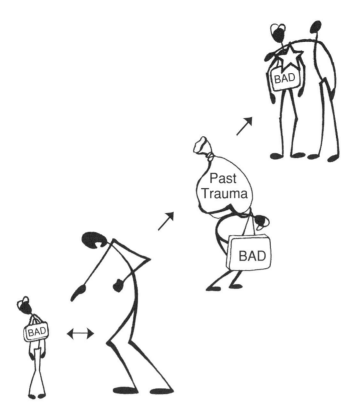

inaccurate self-perceptions. We can learn to question our beliefs about ourselves, to take a fresh look, to adopt a new perspective. We can learn to mentalize, to be aware that our beliefs about ourselves are ideas, many of which we developed early in life. These ideas are not necessarily absolute truths, any more than our ideas about others are absolute truths. These ideas we have about ourselves must be examined and re-examined over our lifetime. Over time, adding new experiences and beliefs adds a positive sense of self.

You may be thinking "This is impossible." And it is true that change, although possible, is very difficult. Even small changes can be tough and not easy to hold onto. Why is this change so hard? Let's take a look at the dilemma of change and what it means to you.

There can be many negative beliefs about the self and worrying thoughts that prompt us to sabotage feeling good. Can you relate to this cycle?

The Pleasure/Guilt Cycle

- Does letting in a compliment or recognition of some aspect of goodness about you stir up fear and guilt in you?
- Are you afraid that if you let yourself feel good about yourself, you are at greater risk for something bad happening?
- Do you feel that you do not deserve good things and that you must punish yourself with self-harm behaviors or judgments rather than letting the good in?

Plan to start by making small changes by thinking or doing something different. You might shift from bad self-statements to neutral self-statements. For example, go from "I'm bad" to "I'm all right," or even, "I'm not always bad." If you try to go all the way from "I'm bad" to "I'm good," the leap may be too great; it's too extreme in the other direction from how you think and feel. Besides, who among us is all good?

Go slowly and take small, step-by-step approaches to recognizing the little ways that you are OK or good. For example,

- "I met the deadline for my project."
- "My eyes are a pretty shade of blue."
- "Sally really seemed to have fun with me today."

When you begin to challenge the negative feelings, thoughts, and beliefs of "badness," you are testing something that leaves you vulner-

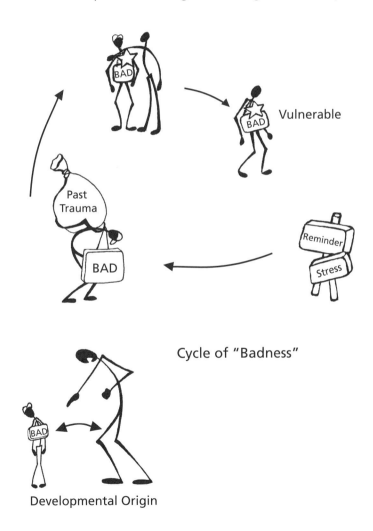

Cycle of "Badness"

Developmental Origin

able and feeling shaky. In this delicate process of change and challenge, if you should encounter more trauma, loss, or acute interpersonal stress, you can easily boomerang back to that experience of "badness" in yourself.

This cycle of taking in positive feedback and nudging your negative self-statements in a positive direction, only to be boomeranged back to a sense of badness when you encounter criticism or stress, is one you will need to repeat over and over to relearn and soften your sense of badness. Working with a therapist to clarify, challenge, and encourage can be quite helpful. Take it in slow and manageable chunks, over time.

Self-Study Questions

1. What biological factors have contributed to your sense of self, both positively and negatively?

2. What social influences outside your family of origin contributed to your sense of who you are today, especially in a positive way?

3. What messages did you receive in childhood that contributed to a sense of badness that you carry with you today?

4. What positive aspects of your current self can you begin to work to accept, slowly and gradually? List at least four positive aspects of yourself you can come to gradually own as yours. Make them believable.

CHAPTER 7

Depression

MINDFULNESS EXERCISE *This exercise involves practice in doing just one thing in the moment. To get ready for it, get yourself something to drink (nonalcoholic of course); a glass of water or juice or a cup of herbal tea would be good. While sitting comfortably with your feet resting on the floor, notice your breath. Do not necessarily do anything to change your breath, just notice it. If you become aware of your mind wandering, just gently bring it back to the present moment. Pick the drink up in your hands. Notice the feel of the glass or mug, the shape and texture and temperature of it. Close your eyes and smell the fragrance of the liquid. Do not hurry yourself, allow yourself to take pleasure in your senses. Take a sip of the liquid and observe its taste and its temperature, how it feels to sip the liquid and swallow it. Repeat this process until you feel more calm and centered.*

We often think of posttraumatic stress disorder (PTSD) as the most common psychiatric disorder resulting from trauma. Unfortunately, depression is also a common consequence of trauma. Depression is a highly prevalent disorder, affecting over 20 percent of women and 10 percent of men in the United States. And depression often leads to significant disability in the form of impaired physical, social, and occupational functioning. Compared with a large number of general medical and psychiatric conditions, depression was the fourth most disabling disorder worldwide in 1990 and is predicted to be the second most disabling by 2020.[1] Although there are many factors that contribute to depression, trauma is prominent among them. Depression and PTSD are similar in that both are responses to unmanageable levels of stress, and both involve high levels of sensitivity to stress.

Why Does Trauma Make Us Vulnerable to Depression?

What are some of the reasons persons with a history of trauma might be vulnerable to depression? Darwin wisely wrote, "fear is the most depressing of emotions." Certainly, traumatic stress is extremely frightening, and many persons feel intense fear in its aftermath, sometimes years later. And PTSD itself involves repeatedly experiencing fear. We think of the relation between fear and depression simply: fear can wear you out. Fear can be demoralizing. By definition, traumatic stress renders you helpless, and the feelings of helplessness and the sense of being out of control can erode your self-esteem and confidence in yourself. When you struggle with symptoms resulting from trauma, your self-esteem is further assaulted. All these consequences of trauma can be depressing. Moreover, like PTSD, depression is both a mental and a physical illness, such that the physiological changes wrought by trauma also can contribute to depression.

Anxiety and Depression

In understanding posttraumatic depression, it is particularly useful to make a distinction between anxiety and depression. We can think of anxiety as the presence of a negative emotion, a high level of

---

[1] Murray, CJL, and Lopez, AD. *Summary: The Global Burden of Disease*, Geneva and Boston: World Health Organization and Harvard School of Public Health, 1996.

distress. Anxiety is largely an anticipatory emotion: we anticipate some future event that shakes our sense of security and competence. Placed on a continuum, we would have anxiety at one end and calm at the other. Perhaps at the highest level of this continuum we would put terror and panic. It's helpful to put depression on a separate continuum.

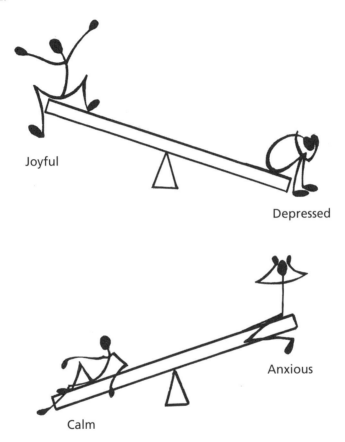

Joyful

Depressed

Calm

Anxious

We would have high positive emotion, such as joy, on one end of the continuum and depression on the other end. Thus, we can think of depression in part as a lack of capacity for pleasure: you aren't interested in doing anything, and you can't enjoy anything, including the things you enjoyed when you were not depressed. Psychologist Paul Meehl proposed decades ago that depression might involve a lack of "cerebral joy juice."

Unfortunately, as we have seen, depression and anxiety tend to go together, so that you can experience the combination of high negative emotion and low positive emotion. In his popular book, *The Noonday Demon,* Andrew Solomon characterized depression and anxiety as "fraternal twins." As Darwin recognized, traumatized persons will be the first to agree.

Antidepressant Medications

For many depressed persons, antidepressant medications are an essential part of treatment, and they have proven to be effective. Helpfully, antidepressants (for example, SSRIs like Prozac®) are also effective in the treatment of PTSD. Yet, as you may well have experienced first hand, although antidepressants may be necessary in the treatment of posttraumatic depression, they may not be sufficient. In working with many traumatized persons struggling with depression, we find that they are saddled with a popular stereotype: that depression is an acute illness, like the flu, from which you should recover relatively quickly. We think of this as the myth of the three-week Prozac cure. No doubt, some persons recover quickly with antidepressant treatment. But that's not the norm. Fortunately, the odds of recovering from a major depressive episode are extremely good. Unfortunately, recovery is often a slow and gradual process. One careful study of patients admitted to major medical centers for the treatment of major depression showed that the median time to recovery (by which half the patients had recovered) was five months.[2] Thus, the cultural stereotype is highly misleading. If you believe this stereotype, you may berate yourself for not recovering more quickly, only adding more fuel to your depression

[2] Solomon, DA, Keller, MB, Leon, AC, et al. Recovery from major depression: A 10-year prospective follow-up across multiple episodes. *Archives of General Psychiatry* 1997, 54:1001–1006.

The "Catch 22s" of Recovery

One reason individuals find it difficult to recover from depression is what we think of as the "Catch 22s." That is, all the things you need to do to recover are made difficult because of the symptoms of depression. For example:

- If you're depressed, you may be urged, "Cheer up! Go out and have some fun!" Yet depression often involves an erosion of your capacity for pleasure. You might try to do things that had given you pleasure in the past, but you can't enjoy them.
- Depression is a response to stress. If you've become severely depressed, it's likely that you're worn out, especially if you are also contending with anxiety. Thus, first and foremost, you should rest and recuperate. Above all, you should sleep well. But a common symptom of depression is insomnia: you can't sleep. Or you may be sleeping too much.
- You should get proper nutrition to maintain your physical health, but you may have little appetite.
- You should be active. Ideally, you should exercise. There are studies that show that regular aerobic exercise yields strong positive effects on depression and anxiety. But depression robs you of energy. You feel fatigued. So it may be hard even to get out of bed, much less go jog or lift weights.
- Others might encourage you to think more positively. Yet, the natural trend with depression is to be pessimistic, focusing on the negative. We have long known that one of the symptoms of depression is impaired concentration and memory, but recent studies have shown that the negative impact on memory is selective. Depressed people do not remember as much that is positive or neutral in content, yet they actually remember more information that is sad or negative than nondepressed people

do. So, trying to think more positively is like swimming against the tide.

- You should socialize when you are depressed because isolation is also a significant contributor to depression, but many depressed persons feel like staying away from everyone.

In thinking about these Catch 22s, it's important to keep in mind that it's difficult but not impossible to recover from depression. Sometimes it just requires an incremental effort to effect change. For example:

- Once you can get yourself up and around, you might focus on gradually increasing your activity, for example, walking out to the mailbox and back, then walking around the block.
- You might schedule activities that could produce pleasure, without overdoing it. Trying to go to a lively party might backfire for many reasons. But you might try more quiet activities that might at least take your mind off the depression for a bit and that might produce pleasure.

Trying to engage in potentially pleasurable activities, while not setting your expectations too high, might jump start those pleasure circuits and get their cerebral joy juices flowing (there are actually a number of them, not just one).

The problems with negative thinking are especially important. When your mood is depressed, you're likely to focus on the negatives—all the bad things that have happened in the past, all the worse things that might happen in the future, and all your faults and limitations. You may be prone to ruminating, assuming that by mulling over your problems you can "think" your way out of them. But lots of research shows that ruminating makes depression worse rather than better.

- If you must ruminate, set a time limit!

When you're depressed, you may also be prone to focusing on global negative thoughts. Global thoughts like "I'm worthless" leave you stuck.

- If you can, focus on more specific problems. For example, saying "I did a poor job on that project because I didn't allow enough time" at least gives you a chance at a solution.

Cognitive therapy, such as described in David Burns's book, *Feeling Good,* is intended to help with such negative thinking. But cognitive therapy should not be equated with the "power of positive thinking." Rather, the challenge is to think more realistically and flexibly. Simply forcing yourself to think positive thoughts that you don't believe may only make things worse. And you may well need the help of other people to orient your thinking in a more realistic way. The key point may be to try to think of alternatives. To repeat, this will often involve a shift from global negative thinking ("I'm a complete failure!") to more specific, neutral thoughts ("I flubbed that interview, but I'll now know better how to handle the next one").

Perhaps more challenging still is coping with the interpersonal aspects of depression. You may be urged, "Don't isolate." This is good advice, because we know that separation, loss, and isolation are major contributors to depression. This is true not just for us humans, but also for our animal kin. Yet, the Catch 22 is that when you're depressed, you may want to be alone. You might feel like retreating to a cave, such as getting in bed, turning to the wall, and pulling the covers over your head. Moreover, if you have been traumatized in relationships, you may fear being hurt again, and you may retreat to protect yourself from additional stress. Yet, the natural solution of withdrawing is not the best, because it perpetuates your depression. Again the motto is to go slowly. It's easy for depressed people to experience a social overdose by going to a gathering with a lot of people who are having a good time. It takes a great deal of energy to keep up a conversation, especially with a group.

- Thus you might do best by engaging in social activities that are relatively low key and don't demand much conversation, such as going to a movie or a concert or a sporting event.

Above all, when you're depressed, it's important to have hope. Yet, one of the symptoms of depression is hopelessness. This may be the ultimate Catch 22. Many persons who are in the middle of severe depression feel that it will never end. You can be so depressed that you can't even remember what it feels like to enjoy something.

- You may well need to be reminded by others that it won't last forever and that you can recover.
- You may need to "borrow" hope from others who are more hopeful about your prospects for recovery until you feel more hopeful yourself.
- You need to keep in mind that depression is an illness, both mental and physical. Therefore, you cannot just recover by an act of will.

To prevent yourself from succumbing to hopelessness, you may need to set your sights on small goals. By small steps, you can work your way toward recovery. And you may need to work on many fronts, such as your sleeping, eating, activity, thought patterns, and relationships. One step at a time.

Self-Study Questions

1. Without ignoring or minimizing the negative aspects of your life, are there neutral and positive aspects of yourself and your life that your depression has been blinding you to?

2. If you have become isolated, who would be the easiest person for you to do something social with, and what would be the easiest activity for you to do together?

3. Think about your sleeping, eating, and exercise habits. Could any of them benefit from improvement (improvement not perfection!)? What small steps could you take to improve your eating, sleeping, or exercise regimen?

4. What in your life gives you hope for the future, even if a faint and distant hope, that you can hold onto until you recover from depression?

CHAPTER 8

Stopgap Coping

MINDFULNESS EXERCISE *Take out a piece of blank paper and something to draw with. Begin to doodle or draw and continue for three or four minutes. Allow yourself to become absorbed in the experience. Feel the pen or crayon in your hand, be aware of its texture and contours. Notice the sound and feel of the pen or crayon as you move it along the paper. Be aware of the sensations in your hand and arm as you draw and the shapes and colors of the lines you are making. If you notice yourself judging how well you are doing or find your mind drifting off, just gently bring it back to what you are drawing. Getting better at being fully present while doing simple things like doodling helps us be more fully present when engaging in more complex activities.*

Many persons who have suffered trauma respond intensely to stress—they have become sensitized. We call this the 90/10 reaction (see Chapter 4).

As illustrated below, past trauma may sensitize your nervous system, then current stressors may put you into an unbearable emotional state. These stressors may include reminders of trauma, adverse life events, or even a stressful lifestyle of running. Once we are in an unbearable emotional state, we want to do something to get out of it, the sooner the better. Seeking relief from distressing emotions is coping. Yet, some forms of coping backfire: they relieve stress in the

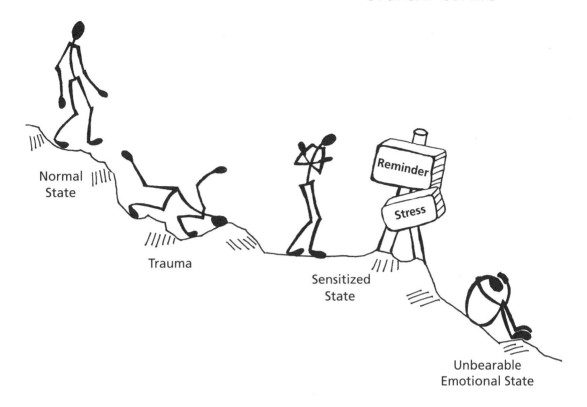

short run but increase it in the long run. These stopgap coping measures have three common features:

- Their primary intent is to positively alter mood.
- They are compulsive; that is, there is a pressure to engage in the stopgap activity, and the pressure is so strong that your ability to control the behavior is compromised.
- They persist despite adverse consequences (things that risk harming you financially, legally, vocationally, socially, or physically—any of which ultimately harms you emotionally).

We distinguish three broad forms of stopgap coping measures:

- Retreat
- Self-Destructive Actions
- Destructive Actions

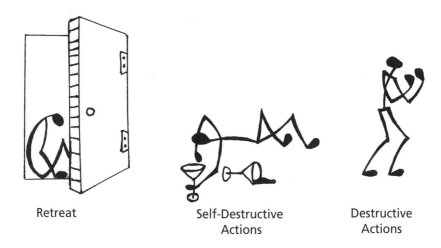

| Retreat | Self-Destructive Actions | Destructive Actions |

Three Reactions to Unbearably Painful Emotional States

Among the self-destructive actions, alcohol abuse is the clearest example of a potentially backfiring way of coping with unbearable emotional states. Alcohol is extremely effective in reducing anxiety and fear. It is fast and potent in producing tension relief. And there is no greater reward than something that decreases pain. Thus, people can easily become addicted to alcohol or other drugs, especially if they are genetically predisposed.

Stopgap measures work, and they work fast! It's no wonder that you may have developed these ways of coping. You use coping strategies that work. The immediate rewarding effect strengthens and intensifies the behavior. The damaging effects often do not begin to show up for quite some time. Thus, you strongly associate the behavior with reward, and you may only weakly associate the behavior with punishment. In the following example, "Susan" starts out using constructive coping methods to calm her anxiety, but because of her trauma history and genetic predisposition to alcoholism, she quickly substitutes an unhealthy stopgap coping mechanism.

"Susan" is in her 40s and has been quite successful in her work as a mid-level manager in a hospital. The hospital, like most others around the country, has been struggling financially. There has been a series of layoffs in a number of the departments in recent years, but Susan has been an excellent manager and has not yet needed to lay off any of her staff members. One day, Susan's boss, Jim, calls her into his office. He says to Susan, "I'm very sorry, but I can't protect your department any longer from the financial pressures affecting healthcare across the nation. Even though you've been an exemplary manager, your department is going to take a **hit**." At this point, Susan's anxiety skyrockets. She lets Jim know that she will need to continue the discussion later when she can be in a calmer frame of mind, and she excuses herself. With heart pounding in her ears and knees shaking, she goes back to her office and tries to calm down. But she cannot get her emotions under control. She tells her secretary she's not feeling well and goes home. She goes for a jog and does some yard work and finally is feeling calm enough by 9:30 to go to bed and fall asleep.

Despite having employed a series of constructive coping strategies wonderfully well, Susan awakens in the middle of the night in a panic. She's had a bad dream about her father. In the dream, she and her sister are little girls again, and her father is drunk and yelling he is going to **hit** them. Then he indeed does begin to hit her sister as Susan stands there helplessly watching.

Again, constructively, Susan turns on the light, goes to the bathroom, and splashes cold water on her face. But she still cannot entirely shake the dream. She goes down to the liquor cabinet. She rarely drinks by herself but keeps alcohol there for guests. She pours herself a small glass of wine and drinks it. She immediately feels a warm and calming sensation spread throughout her body, and she is able to go back to sleep. She has coped effectively.

But Susan's nightmares continue. Before long, she routinely

has a drink before bed to try to stop the nightmares. She has continued to cope actively, but her latest strategy is only partially successful. For genetic reasons, she has a high tolerance for alcohol: she needs more and more to have the same effect. Soon, the wine is too weak, so she switches to vodka. Then she begins to have panic attacks at work, and she decides to keep a bottle of vodka in her desk drawer at the office. Before long, Susan not only is struggling with her symptoms of delayed-onset PTSD, but also is grappling with alcoholism. Initially having helped Susan with her PTSD symptoms, her use of alcohol ultimately makes the symptoms worse. When the effects of the alcohol wear off, her anxiety rebounds. And her alcohol use interferes with her functioning at work and makes her feel guilty, both of which also fuel her anxiety.

Any particular type of stopgap coping behavior may have dramatically positive effects on one person, no effect on a second person, and dramatically negative effects on yet a third person. Of all the stopgap strategies, we know most about alcohol abuse owing to extensive research. If we went out and assembled 100 adults in the community who had never had a drink of alcohol, brought them together into a room and had them each drink a single four-ounce glass of wine, what would we find?

- A few of them would become physically ill; alcohol has a negative physical effect on them.
- Some would experience no effect whatsoever. These are the people who, when drinking a toast at a wedding, take the first polite sip and then set the glass down and do not drink the rest of it. They do not understand why other people drink.
- Some would show a variable response to that single glass of wine: If they were feeling particularly stressed that day, the wine would have a mildly positive effect. If they were feeling pretty

relaxed already, their response to the glass of wine would be much like the second group.

- A few would experience a strongly positive change in mood from drinking a single glass of wine. These are the individuals at high risk for developing alcoholism.

The individuals in the last two groups, those who experience rewarding emotional effects, are at risk of turning to alcohol as a stopgap coping strategy following exposure to trauma.

Other Coping Mechanisms That Backfire

But alcohol and drugs are not the only stopgap coping mechanisms that have negative consequences. Partially determined by genes and partially determined by life experience, individuals differ in their response to various coping strategies. There are common elements, however, to the things these coping strategies provide: powerful relief from tension, a sense of excitement, a means of escape, and a mood enhancer. Examples include:

- gambling
- thrill seeking
- explosive rage
- food (which can be used as a drug in overeating, bingeing, and purging)
- sex
- excessive spending
- deliberate self-harm (cutting or burning yourself, or taking overdoses that are not fatal but knock you out)
- retreat into isolation, depression, or dissociation
- over-work

Let's take a closer look at a few of these and examine the elements of powerful attraction.

THRILL SEEKING

Thrill seeking, such as speeding or engaging in dangerous sports activities, can become a coping mechanism. The adrenaline rush can be used to feel strong and powerful and to combat the feeling of helplessness. Skirting the edge of danger and surviving can give a sense of triumph over the past trauma. Yet, the danger entailed in thrill-seeking behaviors is obvious, and the adverse consequences often contribute to the accumulation of stress pileup.

RAGE

Another way of coping with unbearable emotional states is to explode into a rage, for example, to trash a room. Some traumatized persons adopt the strategy that the best defense is a good offense: they go on the attack. Such aggressive behavior may bring a momentary sense of power that overcomes a feeling of helplessness. Yet, in the aftermath of such an explosion, many persons feel even more out of control and then regret their aggressive outbursts, feeling overwhelmed by guilt feelings or remorse. A common vicious circle is the shame-rage spiral. Consider the following example.

> "Juan" is waiting in a long checkout line at a department store. Unable to tolerate the rising sense of panic over feeling trapped, which is triggered for him by standing in a crowd, he begins to verbally berate and humiliate the clerk for being so slow. Flinging his intended purchase in the clerk's direction he storms off, feeling suddenly strong and free. But by the time he exits the store, his feeling of triumph collapses into a feeling of shame.

SELF-HARM

Harming oneself can reduce tension. It can be a way to express anger (directed toward the self) or combat guilt feelings (as a form of self-punishment). Some persons who resort to self-harm do not feel pain. Their nerves seem numbed and deadened and although cutting or burning leaves scars, they feel nothing. For others, however, the sensation of pain is quite strong and it is just that ability to perceive pain that helps them feel more alive. In addition, focusing on physical pain can be a distraction from emotional pain.

ISOLATION AND RETREAT

Besides the obvious forms of retreat or isolation there are others that should be mentioned, such as spending long hours on the computer searching the Internet or lots of time driving aimlessly about. Both are efforts to lose oneself in activities that feel safe and pleasant and to avoid areas of one's life associated with tension and feeling less in control. Both, of course, can lead to adverse consequences over time.

Such retreats get you out of harm's way. You may feel safer when you are alone because you cannot be hurt. Yet, paradoxically, being alone can also make you feel more vulnerable and therefore less safe. And being alone may evoke feelings of abandonment and neglect, recreating early trauma. Being isolated also fuels depression and deprives you of the opportunity for support, help, and connection.

OVER-WORK

Another form of retreat that is not as obvious as the ones we have just talked about deserves mention: over-working. We have often seen people try to avoid trauma by spending longer and longer hours at work. It is not because the work requires them to do so. Rather, it is because at work they feel in control and better about themselves than they do in any other sphere in their life. Working long hours can be a way to demonstrate their value in the workplace in an effort to counter their poor self-image. They may feel compelled to work overtime even after adverse consequences become apparent, for example, when their spouse and children begin expressing strong negative feelings about their absence.

Self-Destructive or Self-Preserving?

In one sense, thinking of these behaviors as "self-destructive" misses the point. They are efforts to preserve the self rather than to destroy the self. They serve to decrease emotional pain. We think of the main effects of such behaviors as providing relief from tension. Yet, at the same time, these behaviors are undeniably injurious to the self. The scars may be obvious, as in the case of self-cutting. Or they may be more subtle, as in the case of substance abuse, bingeing or purging, or other addictive behaviors. But, over time, these behaviors will damage the body and the sense of self as well as self-esteem. That's why we think of them as self-destructive.

Concern

Support

Anger

Abandonment

The short-term gains and long-term consequences are illustrated in the figure above. Although the main effect of these self-destructive behaviors may be reduced tension, they also have interpersonal side-effects.

Self-injurious behaviors may be hidden from others for a time, but sooner or later they come out into the open and have a strong effect on relationships. At best, other people become concerned and offer support. Such support will be comforting and will add to the relief from tension.

Yet, such concern and support are usually short-lived responses. If the stopgap behavior continues, it is not unusual for others to

- become frightened, alarmed, and angry
- feel helpless and inadequate; criticize
- give up and withdraw.

Such rejection and withdrawal in close relationships is extremely stressful, and it just provides additional fuel to the stress. For example, feelings of abandonment lead to the cycle of unbearable emotion, self-harm, and tension relief, but these means of coping may ultimately provoke abandonment. This is another glaringly vicious circle.

How do you get out of this cycle? As our psychologist colleague Maria Holden brilliantly remarked in one of our patient education groups on trauma, we need to insert a "pause button" into this chain of events. The pause button needs to go in between the unbearable emotional state and the self-harm.

The pause button gives you the space to choose alternative, constructive ways of finding relief from tension. Pushing the pause button gives you time to become aware of your emotional state and the other options open to you. You will be far ahead if you have practiced other options so that you can draw on them quickly when you most need them. When the bear is charging, it's no time to get yourself into

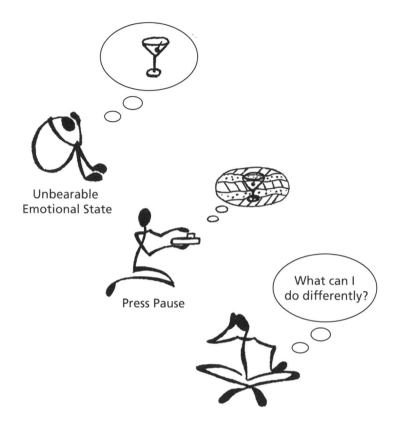

Unbearable
Emotional State

Press Pause

What can I
do differently?

good physical shape so you can run fast! Until you have constructive coping skills, it will be hard to give up the stopgap coping skills you have relied on. We will discuss constructive self-regulation skills in Chapter 11.

Self-Study Questions

1. Have you frequently experienced unbearable emotional states? What feelings do you believe are intermingled to make the feeling state so unbearable?

2. What stopgap coping mechanisms have you been relying upon?

3. What have been the benefits of the stopgap measures?

4. What have been the adverse consequences of the stopgap coping measures on your self and on your relationships?

5. What constructive self-regulation strategies have you developed thus far in your life? Include constructive coping skills you may have had prior to turning to stopgap coping, even though they may have fallen by the wayside.

CHAPTER 9

Reenactments

MINDFULNESS EXERCISE *Sit comfortably in your chair, both feet resting on the floor. Feel the chair beneath you. Notice how solid it is and imagine how kind it is to support you. Feel how solid the floor is beneath your feet and allow yourself to be thankful for that grounding and support. Feel the air enter as you breathe and allow yourself to appreciate that the air is there to nourish you. Then think of one more thing you can be grateful for in this moment.*

In this chapter, we are going to be talking about reenactments—what they are, how they happen, and why they happen. By reenacting, we mean repeating a pattern from the past. We all do this in our relationships. We learn. We generalize from the past to the present and the future. We repeat. Sometimes the past pattern of relating fits like a glove to the current relationship, for better or for worse. Sometimes the fit is not so good, as if we are relating to a ghost of the past rather than the real person in our life at the present. With a history of trauma in close relationships, reenactment is especially problematic: the fit to the present may be poor, and it can bring on more traumas.

Often, despite our best efforts, we find ourselves repeatedly in situations that remind us strongly of a past trauma. This can be perplexing and disturbing and can lead us to feel that we are jinxed. The repetition can make us blame ourselves. As a result, we may feel we are:

- Doomed to be a victim
- Asking for it

It is important that you recognize at the outset that the likelihood of either of these explanations being accurate or true is very small. It is equally important that you not "hear" the discussion in this chapter as confirmation of either of these conclusions.

Lots of these reenactments involve 90/10 reactions: some behavior or feeling in the current relationship triggers emotional reactions from the past. At worst, the 90/10 reactions can escalate into trauma in current relationships. We find it helpful to think of these reenactments in terms of roles: abuser, victim, rescuer, and neglector. We believe that the ordinary, toned-down versions of these roles can be the "10" that triggers the "90" from the past and can lead to repetitions of old, troublesome patterns.

How Do We Reenact?

Ordinary Roles		Traumatic Roles
Hurt	⟷	Abuse
Get Hurt	⟷	Be Victimized
Slight	⟷	Neglect
Help	⟷	Rescue
10%		90%

A number of trauma therapists have observed their clients enacting these different roles in their relationships (Herman, 1992). Sometimes these roles go together like a key into a lock. For example, someone being abusive toward someone being victimized. Usually, there is a neglector or helpless bystander, a person who knows or should know the abuse is taking place but is either blind to it or immobilized in the face of it. Naturally, someone who feels abused, victimized, and neglected will long for a rescuer. Quite often, traumatized children will actively fantasize about being rescued, for example, being adopted by a loving family or even being taken off to another safe planet. And often there is a real person who can fit into this mental slot. This is someone who may or may not know about the abuse but whose kindness tempers the impact. This might be a teacher at school who senses your pain and shows you kindness, or helps you find and express your talents in the classroom. For one of our clients, it was her dog. After being abused she would climb into the doghouse and her dog would cuddle with her and lick her face.

These roles are one end of a continuum of possible relational roles. At the other end are the ordinary interactions, milder versions of these roles. Nearly all of us agree that it is impossible to be in relationships and never get hurt or hurt someone. We are not all cut from the same cloth. We have disagreements, want different things out of life, and get irritable with each other. This is part of life. And we all get preoccupied and end up slighting or ignoring each other at times. And we all like to help each other at times; it feels good to be able to do this. But we mustn't forget that another part of life is learning to ask for and accept help.

Now where on each of these scales does behavior pass from being normal and expected to being potentially traumatic and not OK? How much hurtful behavior should you tolerate? This is a highly personal decision. The answer is different for each person, and for any given person the answer may be different at different points in time. Yet, it is an important question for each of us to be attentive to in our relationships.

Reenactments occur when we and the person we are in a relationship with get too far into the traumatic end of the continuum. As we will learn in the next chapter, compassion fatigue develops when the spillover of past trauma leaves you experiencing yourself as a damaged victim, and your loved one goes from trying to help you to trying to rescue you, winding up feeling exhausted and helpless in the process. But it is not just the victim and rescuer roles that can be reenacted. Any combination of the above can be reenacted in current relationships. A common sequence is this:

- trying to rescue,
- feeling victimized, and
- withdrawing into being neglectful.

We have learned that if you have been in any one of these roles, you will likely reenact all these roles.

Reenactments can be interpersonal or intrapersonal. These intrapersonal reenactments involve your relationship with yourself, which is certainly a most important relationship, because you are with yourself continuously. Intrapersonal reenactments occur when you play these roles out with yourself. That might sound kind of odd at first but we have seen it happen a lot. A straightforward example is this:

"Dante" was yelled at as a child every time he made a mistake. Now he yells at himself, in his mind, every time he makes a mistake. He may use the very same words that he heard as a child. Or the repetition may be subtler, so that he may be unaware of its relation to past trauma. Now that he is an adult, he has internalized both the abuser and the victim role.

Have you ever abused yourself by engaging in activities in part motivated to hurt yourself? Have you ever engaged in thrill seeking so you could rescue yourself and feel the triumph of defeating threatened injury or death? Examples might be

- driving recklessly,
- walking at night in dangerous parts of town,

- repeatedly procrastinating on assignments and then frantically and in an adrenaline rush pulling an all-nighter and getting it done.

Have you significantly neglected yourself, perhaps by

- not eating for extended periods,
- not attending to your grooming and appearance,
- being a workhorse week after week or year after year,
- not allowing yourself any pleasure in life?

If your answer to these questions is "yes" and you are starting to feel shame or guilt, please try to suspend it. When we talk about why reenactments occur it will make sense. But first let's focus on how re-enactments occur.

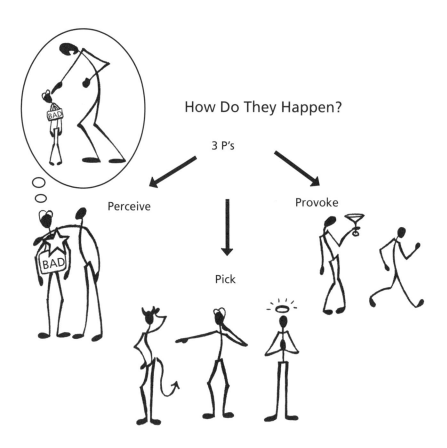

The mnemonic of the 3 Ps can help in understanding how reenactments occur:

- Perceive,
- Pick, and
- Provoke.

In "perceive," normal aspects of life can act as triggers for a 90/10 reaction. An example will help.

"Jane" was working with a young woman named "Sara" who had a history of multiple traumas. In a therapy session, Sara was doing some difficult but important processing of one of her traumas. Jane leaned toward Sara in an expression of interest. When Jane's hair fell into her eyes, she unconsciously swept her bangs behind her ear. Sara suddenly stood up and started for the door. Then she turned back and came towards Jane punching one fist into her other hand and cursing. Jane knew Sara was having a 90/10 and, as calmly as she could, kept repeating "It is OK. I know you feel very scared and angry but there is no danger here now, I am here to help you." Sara left the office and went back to the hospital floor where nursing staff talked with her and helped her calm down. To her credit, she came to her next appointment with Jane, although she was quite wary and guarded. Together they retraced the previous session, trying to identify the trigger. Sara suddenly came to a realization. "I know what it was. When you swept your hand across your forehead. When my mother got exasperated with me and my sister, she would rub her hand across her forehead and then start to hit us."

Once Sara identified the trigger, the past unstuck itself from the present and she no longer related to Jane as someone who was about to hit her or hurt her but rather as a therapist she trusted.

In the perceive mode, the trauma is not actually reenacted, but it feels as though it is.

By "pick," we mean that we can intentionally or unintentionally pick a person for a relationship who is more than willing to participate in reenacting traumatic situations. In some instances, a person intentionally and in a planned way enters into sadomasochistic relationships that involve deliberately inflicting pain. This is one way trauma is repeated. But usually this repetition is unintentional; in fact, it is the last thing in the world the person really wants to have happen. For example,

> "Jessie" is a young woman who lives in a home with an abusive parent. At school she walks with her books in front of her chest, her head down and avoiding eye contact, her hair falling forward to obscure her face. Tony is a bully who is looking for someone meek and docile; he "picks" her. When he asks her out, she is likely to say yes, as she has learned that opposition of any kind makes things worse. When he begins to make rude comments to her, she is unlikely to say, "I do not want to be talked to that way. Take me home immediately or I will call a cab." This kind of healthy assertive behavior has not been modeled or reinforced in her home; indeed, it is likely to have been punished. So, her lack of self-esteem, tendency to freeze, and tendency to be passive in the face of threat, all of which are very understandable given her life history, conspire to have her on a slippery slope leading to a relationship with a young man who is disposed to aggressiveness. Of course, he may be repeating his own trauma, taking the abuser role.

> To explain "provoke" it is easiest to give another example.

> "Mariah" grew up in an abusive home but later married a kind and loving man. When her daughter reaches the same age

Mariah had been when she was abused, Mariah begins to have troubling symptoms. She wakes up frequently with nightmares, which also awakens her husband with a jolt. She becomes sleep deprived and is more irritable. Small things lead her to fly into fight responses where she screams and yells at others and throws objects and breaks them. When her husband touches her, she frequently has an exaggerated startle response and goes into a flight response, withdrawing from him in a panic. Affectionate interchanges diminish and disappear, and then they are replaced by increasing verbal aggression. This ordinarily loving but sleep-deprived man begins to be "provoked" to verbally abusive behavior with his wife. His capacity to remain soothing and calming is diminished; he feels increasingly exasperated by Mariah's reacting to him as being someone he is not—the abusive parent. Yet he is even more exasperated because he is starting to become that abusive person.

Again, remember, we are not talking about either blaming or excusing anyone's behavior; we are working on understanding.

Why Do Reenactments Occur?

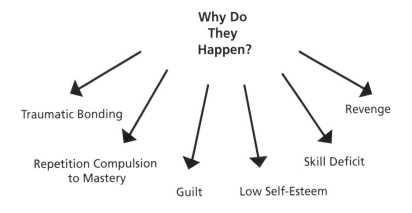

TRAUMATIC BONDING

Reenactments can happen because a person grows up with a destructive pattern of relating and views it as normal. Children tend to think that everyone's experience is the same as their own; it is a reflection of the egocentricity that is a normal part of the way young children think. Another way of saying this is that sometimes these reenactments are built on a pattern of traumatic bonding, that is, being bonded to a traumatic relationship. If you have a relationship with a parent that is alternately loving and abusive, this can be crazy making. That same parent is both an abuser and a rescuer. Paradoxically, the abuse cements the attachment. The abuse is frightening, and the normal response to being afraid is to seek security in your relationship with your attachment figure. A parent who sometimes provides security and other times instills fear can reinforce this traumatic bond. And the greater the fear, the more need for security, the stronger the bond. You may have become so accustomed to this pattern that it feels normal. Then you may find yourself repeating the pattern in other relationships.

To illustrate, we will borrow an example from ethology.

Konrad Lorenz was studying the imprinting behavior of geese. Goslings tend to follow the first moving object they see after they hatch; usually this is their mother. They "imprint" or bond to that object. It is adaptive for babies to imprint to their mother. Lorenz put a doghouse on wheels and rolled it past the hatchlings. They walked quacking in a row behind the doghouse, content and happy. The doghouse fell over and they acted alarmed, shoving at it with their beaks trying to right it again. When Lorenz got it up and moving, their alarm diminished and they again followed behind.

Human babies and children are not as hard-wired as goslings, but there are elements of imprinting in the way we bond to our parents. One client in our group said, "Before I got married I must have dated at least 100 women, many of them were very sweet and nice, but I married the one who, like my mother, abused me." When the other group members asked, "Why didn't you marry one of the nice ones?" he replied, "They were boring." If the early relationships we form in the home are over the top, full of excesses in both directions, then healthy relationships can seem pale and tepid. But, in this case, boring is good.

REPETITION COMPULSION

Freud wrote about the "repetition compulsion" as a form of mastery. Early in his career, Freud's theory was fairly simple. Behavior is motivated by the pursuit of pleasure and the reduction of pain. Libido, the life force, was the driving energy behind behavior, and aggression was the result of libido being thwarted in its pursuit of pleasure. But Freud began observing behaviors he could not account for by this theory. How were the recurring nightmares of devastating war experiences to be explained by the pleasure principle? How was a child, who had been terrified of getting a shot at the doctor's office, pursuing pleasure by giving her dolly a shot while playing later that day? Freud talked about these behaviors, these reenactments of past trauma, as reflecting the repetition compulsion with an effort to attain mastery. It is as if traumatized persons are repeating, repeating, repeating in the hopes that this time they will master the situation and no longer feel helpless and afraid and out of control.

Freud also revised his theory to include two instincts, libido or love (Eros or the Life Instinct) and hate or aggression (Thanatos or the Death Instinct). Not everyone agrees with this theory, but many do. One of the developmental challenges we face is to bring love and aggression into a vital balance, where love constrains hate and predominates over it. Trauma can throw that balance out of whack, leading to poorly controlled displays of aggression directed toward others (interpersonal reenactment) or toward oneself (intrapersonal reenactment).

GUILT

Although we usually know intellectually that we were not the cause of the trauma, at an emotional level we often carry persistent guilt and shame. Why we should carry the guilt and shame when it was someone else who behaved shamefully is a paradox. We may unconsciously hold on to the guilt, subconsciously believing that, if we caused the trauma, then we have the power to prevent it from happening again. Sometimes this illusion of control is worth the pain of the guilt. Yet, the guilt is usually irrational and, furthermore, leads us to believe we do not deserve good things. It may even make us feel we deserve to be punished. Either of these factors can be unconscious contributors to reenactments.

LOW SELF-ESTEEM

Many persons who were mistreated come to feel that they are bad and deserve nothing better. Paradoxically, when they are treated well, they become anxious. They are not comfortable with it and feel they don't deserve it. Then they can retreat to the familiar.

Low self-esteem can lead us to remain in relationships in which we are not being treated well. We may lack the confidence in our ability to have a reasonable chance of succeeding on our own. We may believe that nobody who is nice and kind would want to be in relationship with us. This belief can unwittingly turn into a self-fulfilling prophecy. We may question positive feedback and compliments so much that we never let them in, and others grow weary of trying to give us something we won't accept. We may test the caring of others so frequently that they give up. Then, if and when this happens, it just confirms our conviction that no one nice and kind would want to be in a relationship with us.

SKILL DEFICIT

Imagine that you can answer only Yes or No to the following questions:

- Would you show me how to do a back handspring?
- If I asked you really nicely, would you show me how to do a back handspring?
- Is it because you don't like me that you won't show me?

If your answer to all three questions was No, in all likelihood it is because you do not know how to do a back handspring. Well,

- setting healthy boundaries in relationships,
- learning how to skillfully negotiate conflict in relationships,
- knowing when and how to say "No"
- asking for what we need or want

are no more inborn than doing a back handspring. These are skills we learn. And, while we learn a fair amount from explicit instruction, a lot of what we learn is from modeling or observing the actions of others. If we grew up in an abusive environment, odds are we did not have much opportunity to learn the skills that keep relationships healthy and not abusive. We can end up in reenactments because we lack the skills needed to minimize the likelihood of relationships becoming abusive or we lack the skills needed to terminate abusive relationships. We do not know what we need or want because we have been focused on taking care of others.

REVENGE

In one of our educational groups, we asked the participants why they thought reenactments occur. One woman said, "Revenge." She was admirably brave in bringing this out into the open and very wise to do so as well, given that what is hidden cannot be healed. She went on to say that she had been physically and verbally abusive to friends in her adult life as a form of revenge toward having been physically and verbally abused by an older neighbor boy when she was growing up. Sigmund Freud talked about this pattern as the defense of turning passive into active—turning a sense of helplessness into a feeling of being in control. Sometimes, when we fear something bad will happen, we can try to make it happen to get control over it. You may fear being abandoned and then drive the person away, taking control over the abandonment. And anger can bring a sense of being in control: the best defense is a good offense. Being passively victimized feels awful; being rageful and abusive can feel powerful. Paradoxically, however, the rages often are associated with a feeling of being out of control, so the strategy backfires.

There can be many reasons why reenactments occur. You may know of more reasons, things we haven't learned about yet.

Self-Study Questions

1. Have you ever engaged in reenactments? Were they interpersonal or intrapersonal or both? Do you notice any reenactment patterns?

2. Upon reflection, were the reenactments you just described picked, provoked, and/or perceived?

3. What underlying factors contributed to your reenactments (e.g., skill deficit, guilt, etc.)?

4. What might you do to reduce the influence of these underlying factors?

CHAPTER 10

Compassion Fatigue

MINDFULNESS EXERCISE *Take a moment to become comfortable in your chair, with both your feet on the floor. Relax and take a deep breath, then exhale slowly. Begin with the muscles in your feet and legs. Contract those muscles and hold the contraction for a few seconds, feeling the tension in those muscle groups. Don't contract them too strongly, just enough to feel some tension. Then relax those muscles, feeling the contrast between tension and relaxation. Repeat this process of tensing and then relaxing the muscles in your feet and legs, this time letting the relaxation go even farther. If your mind wanders, just notice it wandering and gently bring your awareness back to the muscles of your feet and legs. Repeat this process by tensing and then relaxing the muscles of your hands, arms, shoulders, neck, and face. Do this again, letting the relaxation go even farther. Feel the tension drain out of your body as you relax.*

Extremes in Relationships

Trauma stems from extremely stressful events in the past that can have significant influences on the way we relate to people now. Most commonly, trauma in past relationships undermines trust in present-day relationships. One diagram that helps us think about the impact of past trauma on current relationships is the Independence/Dependence diagram. This diagram illustrates two extremes in relationships that can stem from trauma: excessive independence versus excessive dependence.

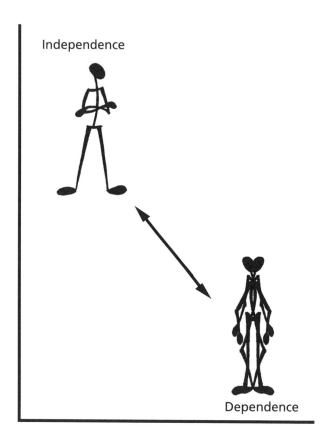

INDEPENDENCE

The extremely independent stance is understandable, given the many ways in which you may have been badly hurt and traumatized in past relationships. At the extreme of independence, you may have a lot of people in your life, but no one really gets in, and you don't rely upon anyone for anything. The advantages of being extremely independent and self-sufficient are that

- you feel safe and
- you gain a sense of competence from taking care of everything on your own.

Like John Donne's poem that Simon and Garfunkel set to music:

I am a rock,
I am an island.
And a rock feels no pain
and an island never cries.

The disadvantage is that over time you come to feel

- lonely
- depressed
- self-destructive
- or suicidal.

We humans are gregarious animals: we are meant to have other people in our lives and to be intimately involved with others. This is a part of our biology and is essential to our survival. Nonetheless, some traumatized persons manage to sustain this independent stance for a long time, sometimes even for years. But extreme independence is a strain and, eventually, the stress may become unbearable. Being extremely independent runs counter to our nature and ultimately may lead to a state of exhaustion, resentment, and depression. With the mindset that we need to solve everything ourselves and never depend on anyone else, we may think of suicide as the solution to end our misery. This is a solution we can accomplish all by ourselves. Suicidal states are the ultimate expression of a sense that others can be of no help.

DEPENDENCE

It is often at this point of suicidal crisis that people enter treatment. Your therapist is likely to encourage you to learn to trust others, to take risks, to open up, and to form attachments. So, you begin to connect, not having had much practice in supportive relationships and not having much confidence in yourself. The anxiety that opening up and reaching out generates leaves you vulnerable to finding just one person to connect with, one person to depend upon. You can then zap over to the other extreme, the extreme of dependence. It may feel as if you have finally found your perfect match, someone who does not judge you, who loves you "unconditionally." You have found the one person among seven billion on the planet whom you can trust. The advantage of this type of extremely dependent relationship is that you feel

- understood,
- secure,
- no longer all alone.

Yet, what usually happens in this type of extremely dependent relationship? If all your unmet needs from childhood, adolescence, and adulthood are flowing into this one relationship, it becomes hugely overburdened. It is not possible for one person to be your mother, father, best friend, spouse, therapist, and caretaker. You sense how burdened the other person is becoming, and

- you live in fear of abandonment and
- you may even inadvertently do things to drive the other person away.

If you fear something is going to happen, you can make it happen in order to feel in control and to get it over with.

One way or another, the other person inevitably ends up feeling smothered or disappoints you in some important way. Then you are left in the very position you have most feared: let down, abandoned, and in need. This state can feel so much like the earlier trauma as to be intolerable. And it is understandable that you then conclude, "See,

I do not do relationships! I always end up badly hurt." Then you naturally go back to the other extreme of independence. It is not unusual to see people with past interpersonal trauma bounce back and forth between these two extremes.

Yet, as we have seen, it is hard to live for long at either of these extremes. Some people manage to do it, but the strain is enormous. Being independent can work for a long time if you're not in need, distressed, or ill. But we all have times of need, and this is especially true of those struggling with a history of trauma.

SELF-DEPENDENCE

We encourage a stance that falls somewhere in the middle, "self-dependence." Psychoanalyst Joseph Lichtenberg described self-dependence as the ability to bridge the gap between separation and re-

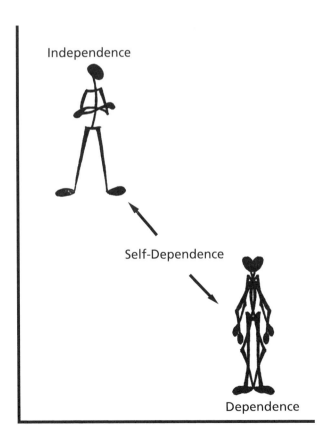

union. He assumed that we all need attachments throughout our life. We all depend on reunion with an attachment figure, especially when we are in pain or emotionally distressed. But we all learn that we can take care of ourselves—for a time. We learn to bridge the gap until we can reunite with our attachment figure. We must bear distress for a while and do whatever we can to comfort ourselves until we can obtain needed comfort from others as well.

Thus self-dependence involves learning how to be alone and take care of yourself. You can enjoy solitary pursuits while also having the capacity to have a range of relationships at varying levels of intimacy. Self-dependence balances alone time with closeness and connection. The set point for this balance differs for each of us, and may differ at varying points in our lives. For example, introversion-extroversion is a dimension of temperament, an inborn aspect of our personality. An extrovert can come home from a social gathering at 11:00 PM and go right to sleep; extroverts get refueled by contact with others. An introvert might come home from that same social gathering and need to read or listen to music for an hour or so before going to bed; introverts are more refueled by alone time. For an extrovert, the self-dependence set point may be more toward the dependent end, and for an introvert it may be more toward the independent end.

But remember: few can flourish at the extremes. Every once in a while you may want to take stock of how you have been living: how much time have you spent comfortably alone and how much time have you spent truly engaging with others? Make adjustments as needed. Don't let yourself remain at either extreme for too long.

Compassion Failure/Fatigue

You may be wondering how trauma, with its potential long-term impact of leading to extremes of independence or dependence, can impact current-day relationships and contribute to compassion fatigue. If you are extremely independent, your family and friends may come to take for granted that you can take care of yourself and that you do not need any help or much of anything at all from them. In other words, there may be a compassion failure at work. They may not realize that inside you feel exhausted, resentful, and silently pleading, wishing they knew just how badly you are hurting and how much you truly need their support, nurture, and practical help.

If you are at the extreme of dependence, you may not realize that your loved one feels smothered, depleted, and straight-jacketed by the relationship until their compassion is so fatigued that they leave you. Or, as we stated earlier, you may be keenly aware of the burden you are placing on your loved one and live in constant fear of abandonment. Psychologist Charles Figley proposed the concept of "compassion fatigue" to refer to the potential for caregivers to become so exhausted that they are no longer able to carry on caregiving. You may become alarmed, or even panicked, as you sense this process unfolding.

Here is something that is very important to understand: We are discussing compassion fatigue not to make you feel guilty or ashamed but rather to help you and your loved ones identify problems so they can be corrected before the inevitable stress of compassionate caring progresses to the point of compassion fatigue, where the caregiver is extremely stressed and exhausted. Our intent is to help you get and keep your relationships on a balanced and healthy path, not to invoke shame or guilt.

VICARIOUS TRAUMATIZATION

How else does past trauma potentially contribute to compassion fatigue in current-day relationships? To understand this process, it is helpful to understand the concept of secondary traumatization, also known as vicarious traumatization. Secondary trauma can happen in a number of ways, one occurring when your loved one moves too far on the Helping—Rescuing continuum we reviewed in Chapter 9. Your loved one may start by trying to help you with your feelings of extreme depression and anxiety but gradually progress to a more extreme position of trying to rescue you from your pain. For example,

> "Kim" was concerned about her partner, "Lee." She started coming home from work during the day to check on him to make sure he was OK. He frequently had nightmares, and Kim found herself losing sleep to stay up with him when these occurred. She stopped exercising and socializing in the evenings and during weekends in order to avoid leaving Lee alone. In fact, she started functioning as if she were Lee's therapist, spending significant amounts of time listening to him talk about the intrusive memories, nightmares, and flashbacks in the hope that listening would make all these symptoms go away. Instead, Kim grew increasingly exhausted and began to view the world as an ugly place.

Rarely does rescuing actually work. All the efforts of the rescuer do not cure you, and these caretakers come to feel ineffectual, out of control, guilty, and helpless—much like you feel in relation to the past trauma. Your loved ones may start to develop many of the symptoms that you have:

- sleep disturbance,
- hypervigilance,
- decreased concentration,
- exaggerated startle response, and so on.

They may begin to develop stopgap coping measures, like the ones we talked about in Chapter 8. Most often we have noticed the loved one relying on

- over-work and
- alcohol use

as a way of avoiding the relationship and containing the spillover of your trauma into them. And, just as it is with trauma, the stopgap coping measures unwittingly worsen the problem of compassion fatigue over time.

And last, your loved one may experience the same alteration in world-view that the trauma caused in you. The world may come to seem to them like a far more dangerous, hurtful, and ugly place than it once seemed. If the trauma you experienced occurred in relation to a family member, your loved one may have the same extremely hard time you have in being around that family member, fundamentally altering the nature of that relationship. In sum, you can see how your loved one may come to experience the same impact of the trauma that you are struggling with even when your loved one may have no personal history of trauma. Of course, with his or her own history of trauma, your loved one may be even more vulnerable to compassion fatigue.

WHAT TO DO ABOUT IT

What do you do if you see signs of compassion fatigue developing in your close relationships? The first thing to do, of course, is to

- give yourself credit for observing these signs and symptoms.

Rather than clobbering yourself for it, give yourself some justified credit for being mindful and observant. Awareness is the first step in a change process; we cannot change a problem we do not even know exists. The second step is to

- talk with your loved one openly and nondefensively about what you are noticing to make sure you are accurately picking up on signs of compassion fatigue.

Then the next step is to

- think together about what needs to be done to help your loved one move out of the rescuer role and back into the role of compassionate helper.
- What do you need to do to take more effective care of yourself and the symptoms your past trauma is causing?
- What does your loved one need to do to take more effective care of himself or herself?

In talking with loved ones of traumatized persons, we found that the single most helpful thing to them was

- taking time for themselves.

Your caregiver is devoted to your welfare. But, just as you do, your caregiver needs space and autonomy. In addition, it is crucial that your relationship involve more than dealing with your trauma. How can the two of you find ways of relating to each other that do not involve caregiving? In other words, how can you re-establish or establish a better balance?

There is that word again, balance. It is one we return to many times throughout these chapters. Finding balance is easy to say and not easy to do. You may feel terrified of decreasing the level of dependence that has developed in the relationship and your loved one may too. That is understandable. Yet finding a balance will enable the relationship to endure, and more than that, to flourish in a healthier direction.

Here are some ways that might right the balance in your relationship. You could:

- sleep in different rooms to avoid both of you being sleep deprived by your nightmares
- establish a broader social network where you each have your own friends as well as shared friends
- find an individual therapist, or together a marital/family thera-

pist, and confine the processing of trauma-related issues to your therapy

- develop healthier eating and exercise routines or outside hobbies and interests

What solutions to establishing a better balance make good sense to you and your loved one?

Self-Study Questions

1. Have you adopted a position of extreme dependence or independence in relation to the significant people in your life? If so, write about what leads you to that conclusion.

2. What effects do you think your extremely independent or dependent way or relating is having on your relationships? What effects is it having on you?

3. Think about the balance between alone time and connections for you as individuals and as a couple. Becoming more aware of these balances and making adjustments to individual and couple's needs can be helpful. What steps do you and your loved ones need to take to find a healthier balance?

CHAPTER 11

Treatment of Trauma

MINDFULNESS EXERCISE *Think of a small task you would like to accomplish today: writing a letter, making a grocery list, sweeping the kitchen floor, sewing a button on a shirt, watering the plants. When you have decided what task you will undertake, go ahead and begin it. The idea is to do it mindfully, with your thoughts focused on the present moment, and not to be judging yourself while you are doing it. If you notice your mind wandering, gently bring it back to the task you have chosen to do. When you have finished, allow yourself a moment to experience the satisfaction of that accomplishment. Try not to minimize it.*

Throughout this book we have talked about ways in which the spillover of past trauma into the present can be highly distressing and at times feel intolerable. It is understandable that once you decide to enter treatment, you feel a high sense of urgency—a need to accomplish everything quickly and to make the pain and the intrusive recollections stop. Historically, the treatment of trauma has followed a straightforward approach that unwittingly supported this sense of urgency. We thought that you just needed to talk about it and process it. That approach to treatment is currently recognized as necessary, but not sufficient.

We find that a significant number of people with trauma-related disorders experience one of two things when they begin to talk about their trauma:

- they feel numb, or
- they feel traumatized again.

Some people talk about the trauma as though they were reading a phone book, detached and devoid of emotion. We find that little meaningful change occurs when this is the case. We would all be pleased if trauma treatment could be painless, but we know that you must, to some extent, feel the fear in order to learn to cope with it. But the other extreme is also problematic: some people talk about trauma and quickly come to feel emotionally overwhelmed, experiencing it as though it were all happening again. Not only is this not helpful, but it can actually be harmful.

We recognize now that the treatment of trauma is more complicated than just talking about it. Currently, we see four necessary components to the treatment of trauma:

- Safety
- Self-Regulation Strategies
- Social Support, and
- Processing

Safety

The first component is safety. By safety we are referring to two things:

- Your physical living situation
- The trust you have in relationships with your therapist and others.

Your living environment must be a safe one. If it is not, the first goal of any change process is to help you create or find a safe living situation. If you are leaving your therapy sessions and returning to a living environment where you are being exposed to violence or other types of threat to your physical integrity and life, your progress will be blocked. The first goal must be finding ways to remove yourself from an environment that is exposing you to ongoing trauma. We are not referring here to ongoing 90/10 experiences but rather to exposure to actual ongoing trauma.

Safety

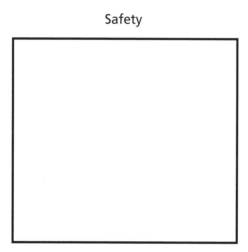

Protecting yourself from trauma can be a challenging goal to meet. Finding the financial resources to move out of a neighborhood where there are drive-by shootings, assaults, and break-ins is not easy. Leaving a relationship with someone who is physically abusing you is not easy; it may take time, and you may need a lot of help. Yet, accomplishing these goals is the first order of business in treatment.

A second aspect of safety has to do with the quality of your relationships with your therapist and others who may be providing professional help. You must have enough trust for these relationships to feel "safe enough," if not completely safe. Of course, trust comes in degrees. You do not need to have total and complete trust in your therapist, and you should not have blind faith in any case. It is healthy and prudent to test the waters in any relationship, including relationships with professionals, as you develop trust. To trust blindly puts you in the position of being overly dependent, as we described in Chapter 10. This stance sets you up for feeling greatly disillusioned when your therapist inevitably does something that disappoints you.

Your therapist is a trained professional, but training does not make anyone perfect. Therapists make mistakes and at times will misunderstand you. Therapists also at times need to help you face things about yourself that are painful, or nudge you to move outside your comfort zone. If you do not have trust in your therapist it will give you reasons to resist this process. You do not need to have total trust, simply the belief that your therapist or treatment team has your best interests in mind. Without this level of trust, it will be very hard for you to form an alliance with your therapist. And the therapeutic alliance is the single strongest predictor of the outcome of treatment. If you do not feel "safe enough" with your therapist, you need to talk with him or her about how you are feeling to see if you can change the relationship. If you cannot come to feel safe and that you are working together productively, you will need to find another therapist.

Healthy Self-Regulation

The second component of effective treatment of trauma is learning and using healthy self-regulation strategies. These strategies are things that you can do on your own to help gain a greater sense of calm and mastery. Without healthy ways of regulating your level of arousal and emotion, you are at risk of resorting to the stopgap measures we talked about in Chapter 8. And, as we discussed in that chapter, although stopgap coping measures are sometimes effective in the short term, they ultimately cause so many adverse consequences that the cost far outstrips the benefit.

In treatment, once safety has been established, we begin to work on developing strategies that help you to manage your anxiety and to take control when anxiety is disruptive. A side benefit is that calming

Safety

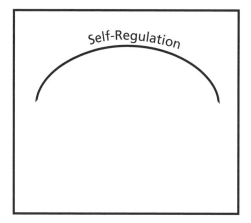

your nervous system helps your mind, body, and overall health. Self-regulation helps to combat and contain the chaos of trauma.

What are some of those self-regulation strategies? The list of potential self-regulation strategies is long. Examples include:

- deep breathing, relaxation exercises, and yoga
- physical exercise and activities like gardening
- music and art
- guided imagery, prayer, or meditation
- biofeedback and self-hypnosis
- cooking and baking
- reading
- contact with pets
- crafts and hobbies

There is no "one shoe fits all." You need to experiment to find the self-regulation strategies that work best for you. In general, you must find an activity that is absorbing, drawing your full attention. Obviously, the kind of activity that you find engrossing will depend on your interests, inclinations, talents, and current state of mind. If you are in a state of high anxiety, the activity will need to be relatively simple, not demanding too much concentration, such as taking a walk. Reading a book or watching TV may not help when you cannot concentrate.

Even though many of these self-regulation strategies are simple, for traumatized persons they can be difficult. There are some unexpected pitfalls. For example, focusing your attention inward during relaxation exercises, meditation, imagery, or prayer puts you at risk of experiencing intrusive images. Similarly, sometimes, trying to relax backfires. If you believe you need to always be on your guard to be safe, relaxing and letting your guard down feels dangerous! You may be surprised to learn that there is a phenomenon called "relaxation-induced anxiety." If this happens to you, try tweaking the self-regulation strategies to make them work for you. Perhaps walking while meditating, or praying with your eyes open will provide just enough grounding to prevent the onset of anxiety. In general, if turning inward leads you to confront painful images or memories, you might focus on relaxing activities (such as reading or walking) rather than standard relaxation techniques (such as closing your eyes, creating comforting images, and relaxing your muscles).

Whatever strategy you use, it is important to experiment to find out what works best for you. The following example will help illustrate:

"Tomas" was using biofeedback for treatment of stress-related migraine headaches. For several minutes, he had been doing standard relaxation exercises, and he had himself hooked up to a finger thermometer. He was trying to consciously dampen his sympathetic nervous system by raising his finger temperature, but he was getting nowhere. Because he was bored, he gave up and started reading, but he left the thermometer hooked up. Then he noticed something surprising: his finger temperature went up. He was relaxing. This was a discovery of sorts. Tomas was aware that he enjoyed reading for many reasons, but he had no idea that he had been using it unconsciously as a self-regulation strategy. It's a good example of a relaxing activity that turned out to work better than the standard procedures for Tomas. It got his mind off worries and problems.

Another way anxiety might be induced is through exercise or other vigorous physical activity. Your breathing rate increases, your heart rate increases, and you begin to sweat. This might feel enough like anxiety to you that it could trigger a panic attack. Or it might remind you of a traumatic experience during which your heart was beating rapidly. You might not even be aware that your increased heart rate is reminding you of a traumatic situation. If this happens to you, try a different type of exercise, perhaps swimming or walking or jogging at a slower pace. Another option is to meet this head on by learning to deliberately increase your heart rate or breathing, knowing that it is exercise and not trauma that is producing this effect. By consciously doing this you may be able to break the connection between physiological activation and trauma.

Just a few words about why pets are included on this list of self-regulation strategies. There have been studies showing that when you pet an animal, its heart rate and blood pressure decrease—and so do yours. Another benefit of interacting with pets is that the responsibility of having a pet can give you a reason to get up and moving in the morning when you might otherwise be tempted to lie in bed and isolate. Sometimes we will do something to take care of our pets that we wouldn't do to take care of ourselves. Helpfully, taking our pet out for a morning walk ends up being good self-care as well.

The trick is to find a number of activities that more often than not make you feel better when you do them. Having a whole range of self-regulation strategies to choose from will make it less likely that you will over-use only one strategy. It will also provide you with options when a particular strategy doesn't improve your mood on a given day.

As one of the members of our trauma education group pointed out, healthy self-regulation strategies work in the opposite way from stopgap coping strategies. The stopgap strategies typically have a powerful mood-enhancing effect the first time we try them. Then it takes more and more to get less and less benefit. The healthy self-regulation strategies, on the other hand, typically do not have an immediately positive impact on our mood. Anyone who has gone jogging for the first time can attest to that! Yet, the more we do them, the more benefit we derive. It takes time to get good at meditation, cooking, jogging, and biofeedback. It takes time to derive their benefits. Yet, ultimately, they can become far more potent and effective.

Social Support

The third component to effective treatment of trauma-related disorders is social support. Consider this contrast: we can do things to comfort ourselves (self-regulation) or we can derive comfort from contact with others (social support). In fact, we believe that we learn to comfort ourselves—ideally, early in life—by having others provide comfort to us. If we have not learned self-comforting from others early on in life, however, we must learn it later. And we are in the

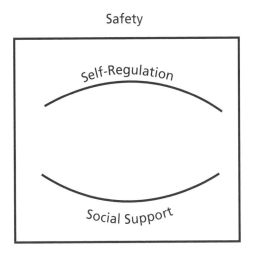

strongest position in coping with trauma if we can do both: derive comfort from others and provide comfort to ourselves. This is the essence of self-dependence, as we discussed earlier.

We understand that trauma often occurs in the context of a relationship—a relationship that, by definition, fails to provide comforting emotional regulation. When the other person both hurts you and is a primary caregiver, this can be a "crazy-making situation" in which no coping strategy works. You are frightened and therefore need comforting, but turning to your caregiver for comfort only increases your fear. Damned if you do, damned if you don't.

Furthermore, learning that others can have a calming effect on you may not have been part of your experience. You may never have observed that relationships can anchor you in the present and create a sense of being part of a caring community. Consequently, you may have exceptional difficulty trusting those you must rely on for caring. We encourage you to start with the people you have trust in right now. Your therapist may be the only one you trust to begin with. Building a trusting relationship with your therapist can be the bridge to building trusting relationships with others. We have been extremely encouraged by our research showing that, despite a history of severe trauma in close relationships, most persons have at least a few persons with whom they feel relatively secure. We also found, however, that some persons go through periods where they feel utterly without trusting relationships. But such relationships can develop, often with the bridge of therapy or some other key relationship.

Think of the network of connections you already have with others: your pharmacist, dry cleaner, hair dresser or barber, postal clerk—all the people you encounter in the places you frequent. These are connections. They are probably not people with whom you will become close. This is OK. Many people make the mistake of thinking that relationships need to be emotionally intense and involve sharing confidences to really count as significant.

This idea struck a chord with "Shawn," one of the participants in our group. He laughed as he told us that he had lost several housekeepers because he wanted them to sit with him for hours as he told them his life story, told them how he was feeling, told them about his latest break-up, and so forth. They were there to clean the house and not to be his confidante or bosom buddy. He realized that he scared them off by trying to create a level of intimacy that was not appropriate to that relationship.

We encourage casual relationships! These relationships are in some ways just as important as the one you have with a close friend or with a therapist. And we encourage relationships at an in-between level of intimacy too: people with whom you play golf or take in a movie a few times a month. Social isolation is a potent depressant. Even brief contacts with familiar persons, for example, the checkout clerk at the grocery store, can provide a bit of a sense of belonging and lessen the feeling of being alone. And, when you're depressed, it can be helpful just to hang out with others in a situation where you do not need to talk much or to confide, such as at a movie or a concert.

Figuring out how much time with others you need is important. This is unique to you. Allowing yourself to feel calmed and secure in a wide range of relationships is the goal. Overcoming a sense of not deserving to be liked and not trusting anyone is the main goal. But go slowly in forming relationships. It takes time to get to know someone. It takes time to learn the ways in which you can trust that relationship. It takes time to learn what you can count on the other for and the limits of the relationship. No one relationship can meet all your needs, and this doesn't mean that the relationship isn't a good and healthy one. Finally, it's helpful to discuss your expectations openly in the relationship when you run into problems. Clarifying expectations can smooth the waters.

Processing Trauma

The fourth component to the treatment of trauma-related disorders is processing trauma, that is, thinking, feeling, and talking about it.

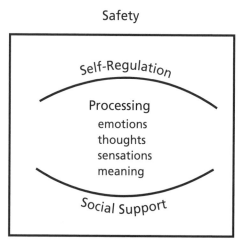

Safety, self-regulation, and social support need to be established before you begin to process the trauma in treatment. They provide the containment for strong feelings that is needed to help you process with the optimum level of emotional arousal: neither numb nor emotionally overwhelmed but rather somewhere in the mid-range. Processing trauma means putting together all of the aspects of the trauma: bringing it to mind, connecting your emotions to the memories, connecting your thoughts with the memories, connecting your physical sensations to the memories, and reworking the meanings about yourself and the world attached to the memories.

The experience of trauma can be fragmenting or disconnecting. Usually one or more of the components just listed have been disconnected from the experience and from the memory. When you connect the trauma experience, it stirs and re-stirs memories of what happened, along with the feelings. Knowing you can regulate your distress or reach out to others for support and thereby anchor yourself in the safety of the present begins to change the impact of trauma on you in the present.

A key element to processing the trauma involves creating a coherent narrative of what happened. Trauma therapists refer to this process as "telling the story." This process of making sense of what happened also entails reworking the meanings that have become embedded in the trauma. By being securely anchored in the present, you can think more clearly and rationally about what the trauma means than you were able to do at the time of its occurrence.

To paraphrase Mark Twain: we should take from life's experience what it has to offer and no more, lest we be like the cat that gets burned by the stove and will never go near anything black again. Think of some meanings often forged by trauma:

- you are to blame or unlovable;
- no one can ever be trusted;
- you are in danger everywhere in the world.

In the process of creating a narrative, you can begin to rework meanings, coming to perspectives that are more accurate and more helpful. These are meanings you can live with, meanings that enhance the quality of your life rather than making life feel unbearable.

Self-Study Questions

1. If you are living in an unsafe environment, what changes need to be made? What people and agencies can help you to make those changes?

2. What self-regulation activities do you already have as part of your skill set? What additional self-regulation skills can you add to that list?

3. What relationships do you have that increase your sense of se-

curity and grounding in the present? Remember to think about the entire range of relationships.

4. Do you need to increase your number of casual or close friendships? If so, how could you go about doing that?

5. If you are in therapy or about to enter therapy, talk with your therapist about how you and she or he can form and keep a strong working alliance. Try to identify specific behaviors that each of you can do to increase the level of trust and alliance in the therapy relationship.

CHAPTER 12

Closure

MINDFULNESS EXERCISE *Sit comfortably in your chair, both feet flat on the floor, your arms resting on the arms of your chair or in your lap. Begin by observing your breathing, doing nothing to change it; simply observing. If you notice your mind wandering, gently bring your awareness back to your breath. Gradually bring your breathing into a slow, easy rhythm that feels comfortable to you. Really notice that each breath draws the air deep within your body. Become aware of the core of your body. Become aware of what is important to you today, in this moment. Allow this awareness to be peaceful, with no sense of urgency or distress.*

Sometimes finishing a book feels bittersweet. On the one hand, there is a sense of accomplishment and mastery in completing something and in learning new things that help to make sense of your experience. On the other hand, there is a sense of disappointment and loss that one has reached an ending. And we have reached an ending of sorts. We are soon to be ending the verbal and visual dialogue we have had together over the past several chapters.

Yet, as is true for many endings in life, the process that was started does not end, even though the concrete aspects of the relationship do end. Think of the teachers, friends, mentors you have had over the course of your life, people with whom you no longer actually have any contact. Those relationships have had an enduring influence on who you are and how you live. It is our hope that your relationship with us through the medium of this book will have an enduring impact on who you are becoming and how you live.

Mastering trauma is a lifelong process rather than a single momentous accomplishment. It entails making at times subtle and yet profoundly meaningful lifestyle changes: changes in how you think about yourself, how you relate to others, how you cope with stress and adversity.

At times you will feel resentment at having to engage in the effortful process of change. You are the one who was injured, and yet you are the one who must put the effort into healing and mastering the ongoing damage of the trauma. It is not fair; it ought not to have happened. And yet the alternative to putting the effort into mastering the trauma is not fair or desirable either.

Feeling and constructively expressing "righteous" anger is part of the recovery process, but try not to dwell too long in a place of bitterness. Episodic bursts of outrage are natural, but ongoing hostility and resentment may lock you into the identity of being a helpless victim—the very role from which you are trying to emerge.

We have provided in this book a kind of road map or blueprint for the process of gradually obtaining mastery. Change is slow and often hard won. And it is possible. In that recognition, there is hope. It is very important that you notice the small signs of growth that you make—accepting a compliment rather than automatically discounting it, taking a walk or listening to music rather than engaging in old stopgap coping behaviors, setting a healthy boundary rather than passively going along with something you find objectionable.

Recognizing these small signs of growth builds a healthy sense of pride and agency. By agency, we mean the experience of being an agent capable of constructive action in life rather than a person who is passively buffeted by the forces around and within him or her. When we have evidence that our problem-solving actions really can solve problems, really can create an increased sense of mastery, we earn one of the greatest gifts of all: the gift of hope. We hope that reading this book and completing the mindfulness and homework exercises have helped you set in motion a process of change in your thinking and behavior that will restore your hope for your future. We wish you well on your journey.

Glossary

ABUSER: a person whose behavior threatens another person's or animal's life or physical integrity. A possible role in the reenactments of trauma dynamics.

ADRENALINE: a chemical compound secreted by the adrenal glands and conveyed to other organs by the blood stream.

ADRENOCORTICOTROPHIC HORMONE or ACTH: a pituitary hormone that causes the adrenal glands to secrete adrenaline and glucocorticoids.

ALPHA MALE: dominant male, "the leader of the pack."

AMYGDALA: a brain structure that plays a role in a particular kind of learning, especially in situations that are threatening and cause fear.

AROUSAL, PHYSIOLOGICAL: the effect of the nervous system on the body generally when it faces the demand for work, such as would be required to fight or flee. The increased ability to engage in work is reflected in increased heart rate, breathing rate, muscle tension and strength, and so on.

ATTUNEMENT: sensing or being in harmony with another living thing's feelings and thoughts with reasonable accuracy.

AUTONOMIC NERVOUS SYSTEM (ANS): a branch of the nervous system that regulates the glands and organs.

BIOFEEDBACK: Training designed to develop one's ability to control the autonomic nervous system; used as one possible treatment option for anxiety and PTSD.

CARNIVORES: meat eaters.

CATCH 22: being caught in the bind of not being able to do things in order to overcome a problem *because* of the problem; for example, in depression, being unable to socialize, exercise, or do other things that will help improve mood because of a depressed mood.

CENTRAL NERVOUS SYSTEM AROUSAL. *See* Arousal, physiological

CEREBRAL JOY JUICE: dopamine, one of the neurotransmitters in the brain. Neurotransmitters are the chemicals neurons release to communicate with each other.

COMBAT FATIGUE: terms used years ago to refer to PTSD caused by combat experience. Also known as combat neurosis and/or shell shock

COMBAT NEUROSIS: terms used years ago to refer to PTSD caused by combat experience. Also known as combat fatigue and/or shell shock.

COMPASSION FATIGUE: a deep awareness of the trauma, pain, and suffering of others to the point where the helper experiences secondary or vicarious traumatization. (From Charles Figley's definition: "the natural consequent behaviors and emotions resulting from knowing about a traumatizing event experienced by a significant other—the stress resulting from helping or wanting to help a traumatized or suffering person.") *See also* Traumatization, secondary or vicarious

CORTEX: literally means bark or covering. The cortex is the cell bodies of neurons arranged in layers on the surface of the brain.

DOSE-RESPONSE EFFECT: the more severe the traumatic events a person is exposed to, or the more numerous, the greater the likelihood that an individual will develop symptoms of a psychiatric disorder.

EGOCENTRIC: viewing events as caused by or referring to oneself.

ETHOLOGY: the scientific study of animal behavior.

EROS or the LIFE INSTINCT: the instinct that is expressed in loving, constructive, and procreative acts.

EXISTENTIAL PSYCHIATRY: the branch of psychiatry devoted to studying how people create meaning in their lives.

FIGHT/FLIGHT/FREEZE: potentially adaptive responses in the face of traumatic events.

FLASHBACKS: experience of a past event, usually a traumatic one, happening all over again in the present.

FLOPPY IMMOBILITY: a potentially adaptive response in the face of a life-threatening situation.

GYRI: the humps in the cortex of the brain.

HIPPOCAMPUS: a brain structure that helps to lay down new memories.

HYPERVIGILANCE: senses on high alert.

HYPOTHALAMUS: a brain structure that controls the autonomic nervous system.

INFUNDIBULUM: the stalk that connects the pituitary gland to the hypothalamus.

INTRA-PERSONAL: within the individual or self; a person's relationship with him or herself.

J P FLAGS: an acronym to help remember basic feelings of joy, pain, fear, loneliness, anger, guilt, and shame.

LIMBIC SYSTEM: structures deep in the brain that human beings share in common with many other animals. These structures play a role in emotions and drives.

MASTERY: competence or effectiveness; exerting the right level of control of oneself and the environment.

MENTALIZING: being aware of mental states, such as desires, feelings, and beliefs, in oneself and others.

MINDFULNESS: the practice of keeping one's mind as fully present in the moment as possible, noticing when one's mind leaves the present moment or become judgmental, and returning one's mind to the present.

NEGLECT, SEVERE: failure to meet basic needs for food, clothing, supervision, and shelter to the extent that physical well-being is endangered.

NEGLECTOR: someone who knows that abuse is occurring but does not take action to prevent it, for any number of reasons. A possible reenactment role in trauma dynamics.

NERVOUS SYSTEM:

Autonomic nervous system (ANS): a branch of the nervous system that regulates glands and organs.

Parasympathetic branch: the branch of the ANS that decreases activity of glands and organs.

Sympathetic branch: the branch of the ANS that increases activity.

NEUROANATOMY: the physical structure and function of the nervous system.

NEUROPHYSIOLOGY: the contribution of the nervous system to how the body functions.

NEUROPSYCHOLOGICAL TESTING: Question and answer, paper and pencil, and performance tests that assess the functions performed by the brain. These functions include, but are not limited to, talking, spatial orientation, planning, and perceiving.

90/10 REACTIONS: the experience of 10 percent of current reality being similar enough to a past trauma that it pulls 90 percent of the past reality into the present and makes a person react like it is all happening again (100 percent). A helpful concept to gain distance from the emotional reaction caused by sensitivity and to assist in mentalizing; "I'm in a 90/10 right now"; "I'm reacting too strongly to what is occurring."

OMNIVORES: meat and plant eaters.

PARASYMPATHETIC BRANCH: *See* Nervous system

PAUSE BUTTON: the capacity to mentalize in between an event and an emotionally driven reaction.

PHYLOGENETIC: referring to the evolution or development of a species.

PHYSIOLOGICAL AROUSAL: the effect of the nervous system on the body generally when it faces the demand for work, such as would be required to fight or flee. The increased ability to engage in work is reflected in increased heart rate, breathing rate, muscle tension and strength, and so on.

PITUITARY GLAND: a gland at the base of the brain that stores and secretes hormones.

POINT OF DIFFICULT RETURN: the point in the gradual buildup of intensity of any emotion from which it takes great effort to calm down to a normal baseline or to be able to mentalize.

POSTTRAUMATIC STRESS DISORDER (PTSD): a cluster of symptoms and experiences that develop after exposure to a traumatic event that cause significant distress or impairment of daily life functioning.

REENACTMENT: when the past is repeated in a present relationship.

RELAXATION-INDUCED ANXIETY: the feeling of fear some people experience when they let their guard down and relax.

REPETITION COMPULSION: the compulsion to repeat in the hope of obtaining mastery.

RESCUER: a person who rescues another from abuse. A possible role in the reenactment of trauma dynamics.

RESILIENCE: the ability to recover from or adapt to change and adversity.

RESTING LEVEL OF ACTIVATION: the level of physiological arousal present when a person is at rest.

SECONDARY TRAUMATIZATION. *See* Traumatization, secondary or vicarious

SELF-DEPENDENCE: the ability to bridge the gap between separation and reunion.

SENSITIZATION or KINDLING: a process where the threshold for firing of a set of neurons becomes lowered.

SHELL SHOCK: terms used years ago to refer to PTSD caused by combat experience. Also known as combat neurosis or combat fatigue.

SOCIAL SUPPORT: the actions of others that make one feel secure.

STOPGAP COPING MECHANISMS: activities engaged in with the primary intent of making us feel better; activities that become compulsive or driven and persist despite bad consequences.

SULCI: the valleys in the cortex of the brain.

SYMPATHETIC BRANCH. *See* Nervous system

TEMPERAMENT: the aspects of personality people are born with.

TRAUMA: lasting negative effects of events that threaten or cause physical harm and provoke feelings of terror and helplessness.

TRAUMATIZATION, SECONDARY OR VICARIOUS: a process where a person who listens to and supports someone with trauma may develop symptoms of PTSD even in the absence of a personal trauma history. (From Charles Figley's definition: "the natural consequent behaviors and emotions resulting from knowing about a traumatizing event experienced by a significant other—the stress resulting from helping or wanting to help a traumatized or suffering person.") *See also* Compassion fatigue

THANATOS or the DEATH INSTINCT: the instinct that expresses itself in aggression and destructive behavior.

TRAUMATIC BONDING: an enduring emotional attachment to someone who is abusive; an attachment pattern that can contribute to reenactment of past abuse in subsequent relationships; the "crazy making" experience where the same person who cares for someone also abuses them.

VICTIM: a person or animal whose life or physical integrity is placed in danger. A possible role in the reenactments of trauma dynamics.

Bibliography

Allen, J. G. (2001). *Traumatic relationships and serious mental disorders.* Chichester, UK: Wiley.

Allen, J. G. (2002). Coping with the catch 22s of depression: A guide for educating patients. *Bulletin of the Menninger Clinic, 66,* 103–144.

Allen, J. G., Huntoon, J., Fultz, J., Stein, H., Fonagy, P., & Evans, R. B. (2001). A model for brief assessment of attachment and its application to women in inpatient treatment for trauma-related psychiatric disorders. *Journal of Personality Assessment, 76,* 421–447.

American Psychiatric Association (2000). *Diagnostic and statistical manual of mental disorders, fourth edition, text revision (DSM-IV-TR).* Washington, DC: American Psychiatric Press.

Beattie, M. (1990). *The language of letting go.* New York, NY: MJF Books.

Bifulco, A., & Moran, P. (1998). *Wednesday's child: Research into women's experience of neglect and abuse in childhood, and adult depression.* London: Routledge.

Bowlby, J. (1988). *A secure base: Parent-child attachment and healthy human development.* New York: Basic Books.

Darwin, C. (1872/1965) *The expression of emotion in man and animals.* Chicago: University of Chicago Press.

Foa, E. B., & Rothbaum, B. O. (1998). *Treating the trauma of rape: Cognitive behavioral therapy for PTSD.* New York: Guilford.

Figley, C. R. (Ed.) (1995). *Compassion fatigue: Coping with secondary traumatic stress disorder in those who treat the traumatized.* New York: Brunner/Mazel.

Fonagy, P., Gergely, G., Jurist, E. L., & Target, M. *Affect regulation, mentalization, and the development of the self.* New York: Other Press.

Frankl, V. E. (1962). *Man's search for meaning.* Boston: Beacon Press.

Freud, S. (1920) *Beyond the pleasure principle.* Vol. 18 in *The Standard edition of the complete psychological works of Sigmund Freud,* ed. James Strachey. London: Allen and Unwin, 1955.

Horwitz, M. J. (1997). *Stress response syndromes: PTSD, grief, and adjustment disorders* (3rd ed.). Northvale, NJ: Aronson.

Kagan, J., & Snidman, N. (1991) Temperamental factors in human development. *American Psychologist, 46,* 856–862.

Kluft, R. P. (1993). Basic principles in conducting the psychotherapy of multiple personality disorder. In R. P. Kluft & C. G. Fine (Eds.), *Clinical perspectives on multiple personality disorder* (pp. 19–50). Washington, DC: American Psychiatric Press.

Linehan, M. M. (1993). *Skills training manual for treating borderline personality disorder.* New York, NY: The Guilford Press.

Lichtenberg, J. D. (1989). *Psychoanalysis and motivation.* Hillsdale, NJ: Analytic Press.

Lorenz, K. (1952). *King Solomon's ring.* New York, NY: Thomas Y. Crowell.

Meehl, P. E. (1975). Hedonic capacity: Some conjectures. *Bulletin of the Menninger Clinic, 39,* 295–307.

Maclean, P. D. (1955). The limbic system ("visceral brain") in relation to central grey and reticulum of the brain stem. *Psychosomatic Medicine, 17,* 355–366.

Pepping, M. (1993). Transference and countertransference issues in brain injury rehabilitation: Implications for staff training. In C. J. Durgin, N. D. Schmidt, & L. J. Fryer (Eds.) *Staff development and clinical intervention in brain injury rehabilitation* (pp. 87–104). Gaithersburg, MD: Aspen.

Stein, H., Allen, J. G., & Hill, J. (2003). Roles and relationships: A psychoeducational approach to reviewing strengths and difficulties in adulthood functioning. *Bulletin of the Menninger Clinic, 67,* 281–313.

van der Kolk, B. A. (1989). The compulsion to repeat the trauma: Reenactment, revictimization, and masochism. *Psychiatric Clinics of North America, 12,* 389–411.

Suggested Readings

Adams, K. (1998). *The way of the journal: a journal therapy workbook for healing.* 2nd ed. Baltimore: Sidran Institute Press.

Allen, J. G. (2005). *Coping with trauma: Hope through understanding.* Washington, DC: American Psychiatric Publishing.

Benson, H. (1975). *The relaxation response.* New York: Avon.

Burns, D. D. (1980). *Feeling good: The new mood therapy.* New York: William Morrow.

Cohen, B.M., Barnes, M., and Rankin, A. (1995). *Managing traumatic stress through art: Drawing from the center.* Baltimore: Sidran Institute Press.

Dubovsky, S. L. (1997). *Mind-body deceptions: The psychosomatics of everyday life.* New York: Norton.

Herman, J. L. (1992). *Trauma and recovery.* New York: Basic Books.

Hanh, T. N. (1991). *Peace is every step: The path of mindfulness in everyday life.* New York: Bantam.

Hanh, T. N. (1987). *The miracle of mindfulness: A manual on meditation.* Boston. Beacon Press.

Harris, M. (2004). *The twenty-four carat Buddha and other fables: Stories of self-discovery.* Baltimore: Sidran Institute Press.

Janoff-Bulman, R. (1992). *Shattered assumptions: Toward a new psychology of trauma.* New York: Free Press.

Kabat-Zinn, J. (1990). *Full catastrophe living: Using the wisdom of your body and mind to face stress, pain and illness.* New York: Delacorte Press.

Kabat-Zinn, J. (1994). *Wherever you go, there you are: Mindfulness meditation in everyday life.* New York: Hyperion.

Matsakis, A. (1996). *Vietnam wives: Facing the challenges of life with veterans suffering post-traumatic stress.* Baltimore: Sidran Institute Press.

Terr, L. (1940). *Unchained memories: True stories of traumatic memories, lost and found.* New York. Basic Books.

Vermilyea, E. (2000). *Growing beyond survival: A self-help toolkit for managing traumatic stress.* Baltimore: Sidran Institute Press.

Whybrow, P. (1997). *A mood apart.* New York: Basic Books.

Zerbe, K. J. (1993). *The body betrayed: Women, eating disorders and treatment.* Washington, DC: American Psychiatric Press.

Index

ABOUT THE **S** SIDRAN INSTITUTE

The Sidran Institute, a leader in traumatic stress education and advocacy, is a nationally focused nonprofit organization devoted to helping people understand, manage, and treat traumatic stress. Our education and advocacy promotes greater understanding of:

- The early recognition and treatment of trauma-related stress in children;
- The understanding of trauma and its long-term effect on adults;
- The strategies leading to greatest success in self-help recovery for trauma survivors;
- The clinical methods and practices leading to greatest success in aiding trauma victims;
- The development of public policy initiatives that are responsive to the needs of adult and child survivors of traumatic events.

To further this mission, Sidran operates the following programs:

THE SIDRAN INSTITUTE PRESS publishes books and educational materials on traumatic stress and dissociative conditions. A recently published example is *Growing Beyond Survival: A Self-Help Toolkit for Managing Traumatic Stress,* by Elizabeth Vermilyea. This innovative workbook provides skill-building tools to empower survivors to take control of their trauma symptoms.

Some of our other titles include *Risking Connection: A Training Curriculum for Working with Survivors of Childhood Abuse* (a curriculum for mental health professionals and paraprofessionals), *Managing Traumatic Stress Through Art* (an interactive workbook to promote healing), and *The Twenty-Four Carat Buddha and Other Fables: Stories of Self-Discovery.*

THE SIDRAN BOOKSHELF ON TRAUMA AND DISSOCIATION is an annotated mail order and web catalog of the best in clinical, educational, and survivor-supportive literature on post-traumatic stress, dissociative conditions, and related topics.

THE SIDRAN RESOURCE CENTER—drawing from Sidran's extensive database and library—provides information and resources at no cost to callers from around the English-speaking world. The information includes: trauma-experienced therapists, traumatic stress organizations, educational books and materials, conferences, trainings, and treatment facilities.

SIDRAN TRAINING AND CONSULTATION SERVICES provide conference speakers, pre-programmed and custom workshops, consultation, and technical assistance on all aspects of traumatic stress including:

- PUBLIC EDUCATION AND CONSULTATION to organizations, associations, and government on a variety of trauma topics and public education strategies.
- AGENCY TRAINING on trauma-related topics, such as Trauma Symptom Management, Assessment and Treatment Planning, Borderline Personality Disorder, and others. We will be glad to customize presentations for the specific needs of your agency.
- SURVIVOR EDUCATION programming including how to start and maintain effective peer support groups, community networking for trauma support, successful selection of therapists, coping skills, and healing skills.

For more information on any of these programs and projects, please contact us:

Sidran Institute
200 East Joppa Road, Suite 207, Baltimore, MD 21286
Phone: 410-825-8888   Fax: 410-337-0747
E-mail: sidran@sidran.org   Website: www.sidran.org

About the Authors

LISA LEWIS and JON G. ALLEN are Senior Psychologists at The Menninger Clinic. Dr. Lewis is Associate Professor in The Menninger Department of Psychiatry and Behavioral Sciences at the Baylor College of Medicine in Houston, Texas. Dr. Allen is Professor of Psychiatry and Helen Malsin Palley Chair in Mental Health Research, Menninger Department of Psychiatry and Behavioral Sciences at the Baylor College of Medicine in Houston. KAY KELLY was the former Director of Social Work at The Menninger Clinic in Topeka, Kansas, and is a cofounder of and clinical social worker at the Heritage Mental Health Clinic in Topeka.